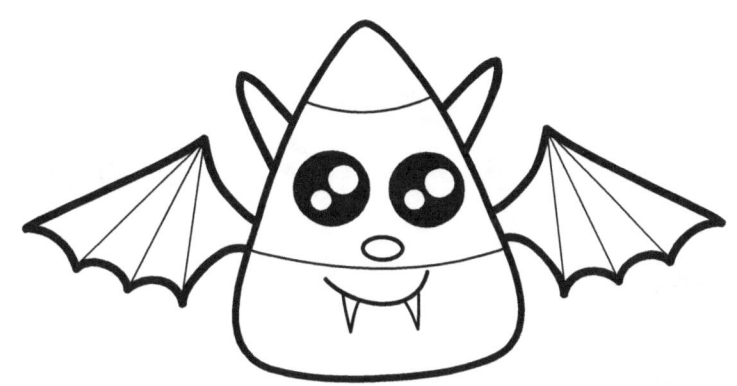

A coloring adventure for all

Jeanette Wummel

Coloring Tip:

When coloring with markers place a piece of paper between pages to prevent bleeding to your next design.

Acknowledgments

Halloween is one of my favorite times of year. This book is dedicated to all those who can never get enough Halloween. Thank you for being you and never change. I would like to give a big thank you to all the people who have supported and encouraged me in making my dreams come true.

Follow me

Website/Blog:
www.TheRootsofDesign.com

Facebook:
www.facebook.com/TheRootsofDesign

Facebook Group:
www.facebook.com/group/ColoringRoots

Instagram:
www.instagram.com/therootsofdesign

Twitter:
https://twitter.com/Roots_Of_Design

Etsy:
www.RootsDesign.Etsy.com

Patreon:
www.patreon.com/RootsOfDesign

Copyright

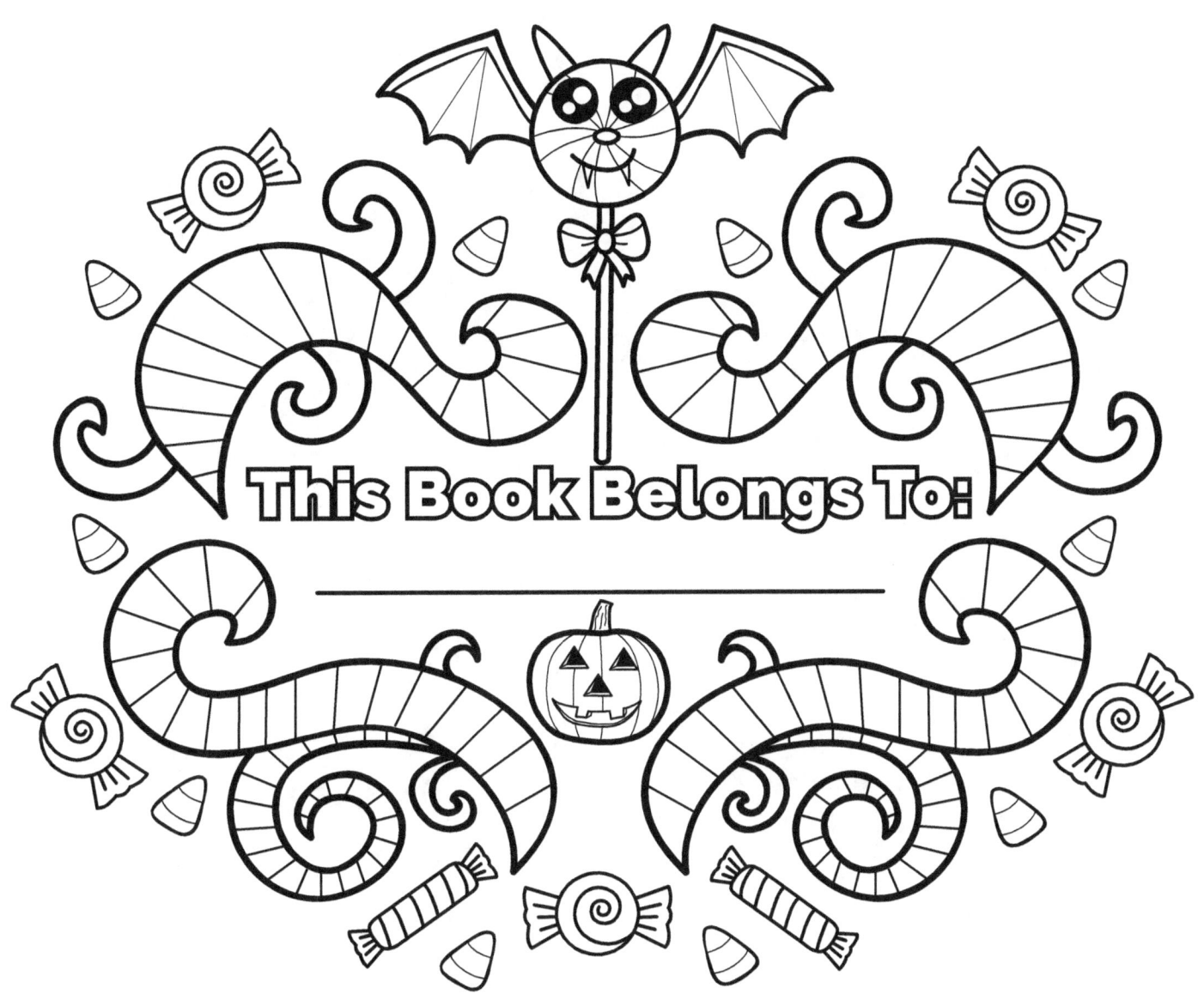

This Book Belongs To:

_____

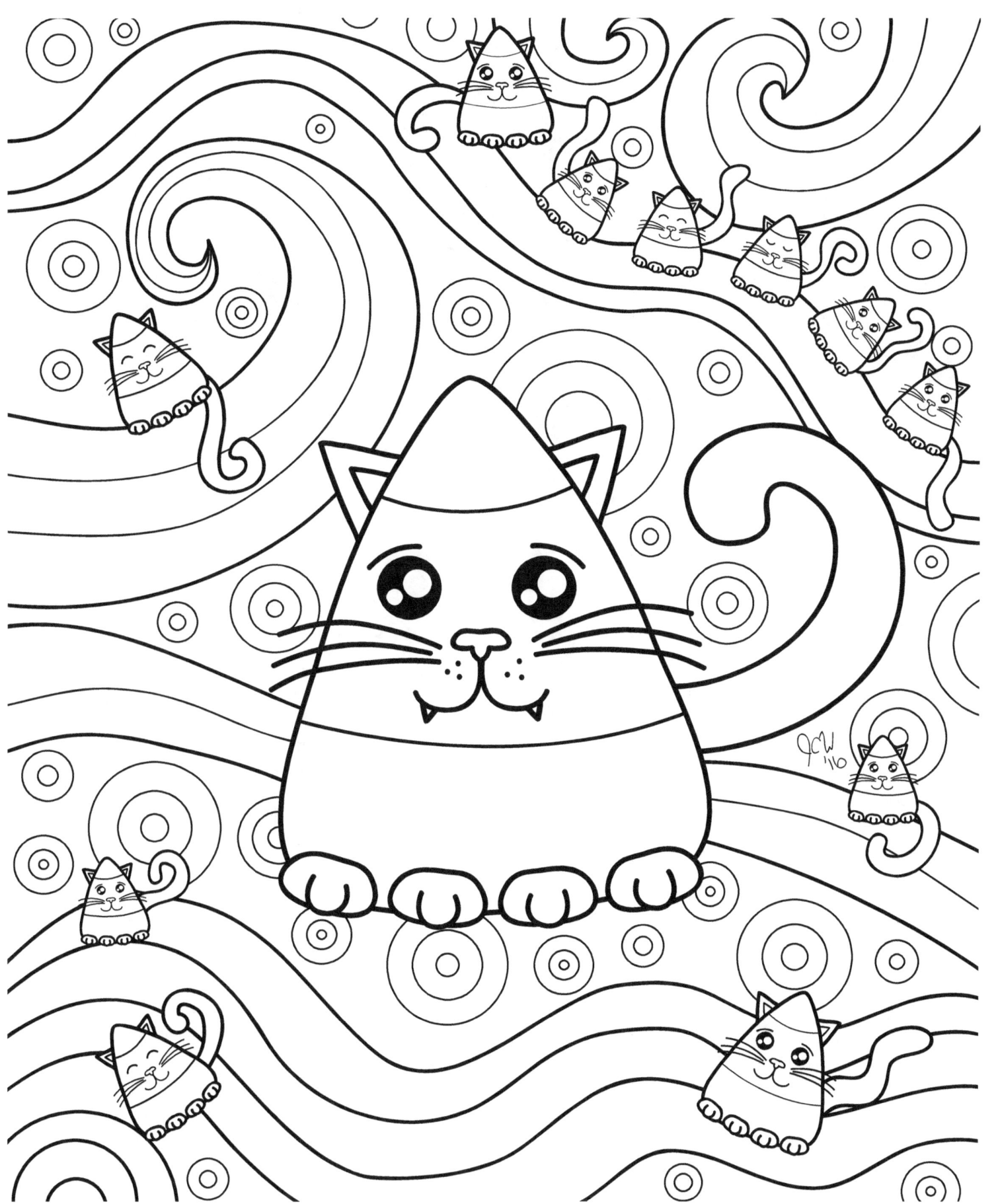

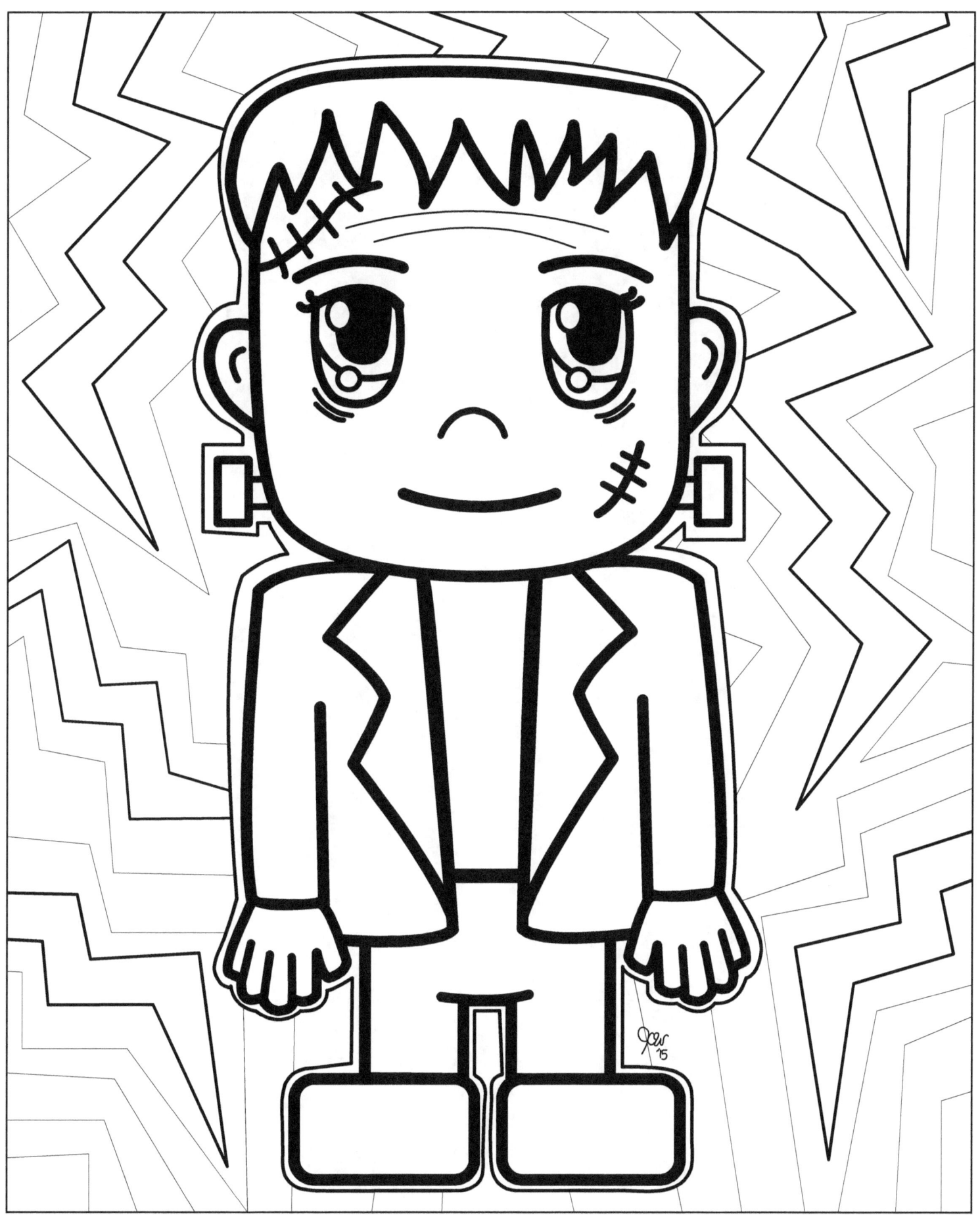

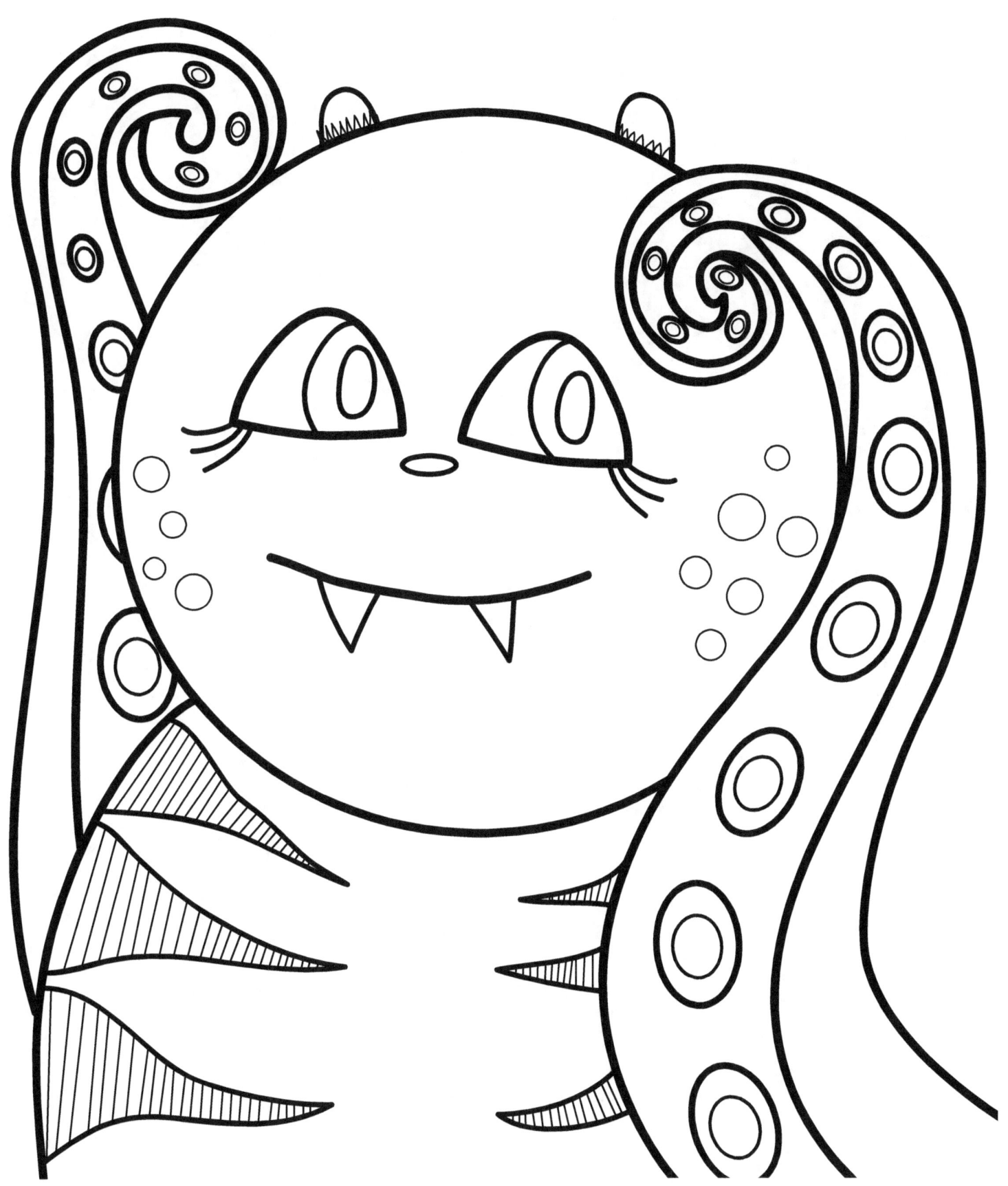

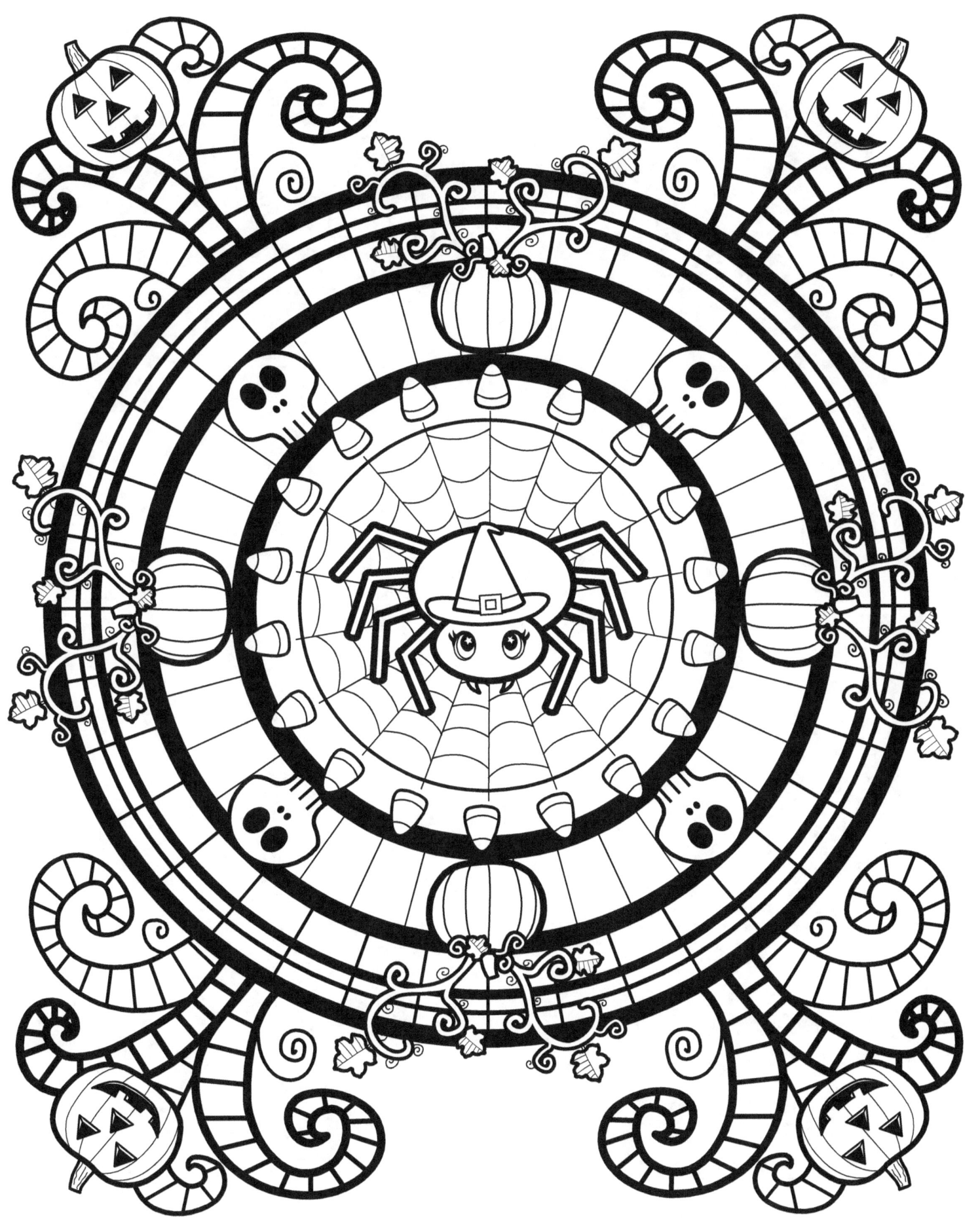

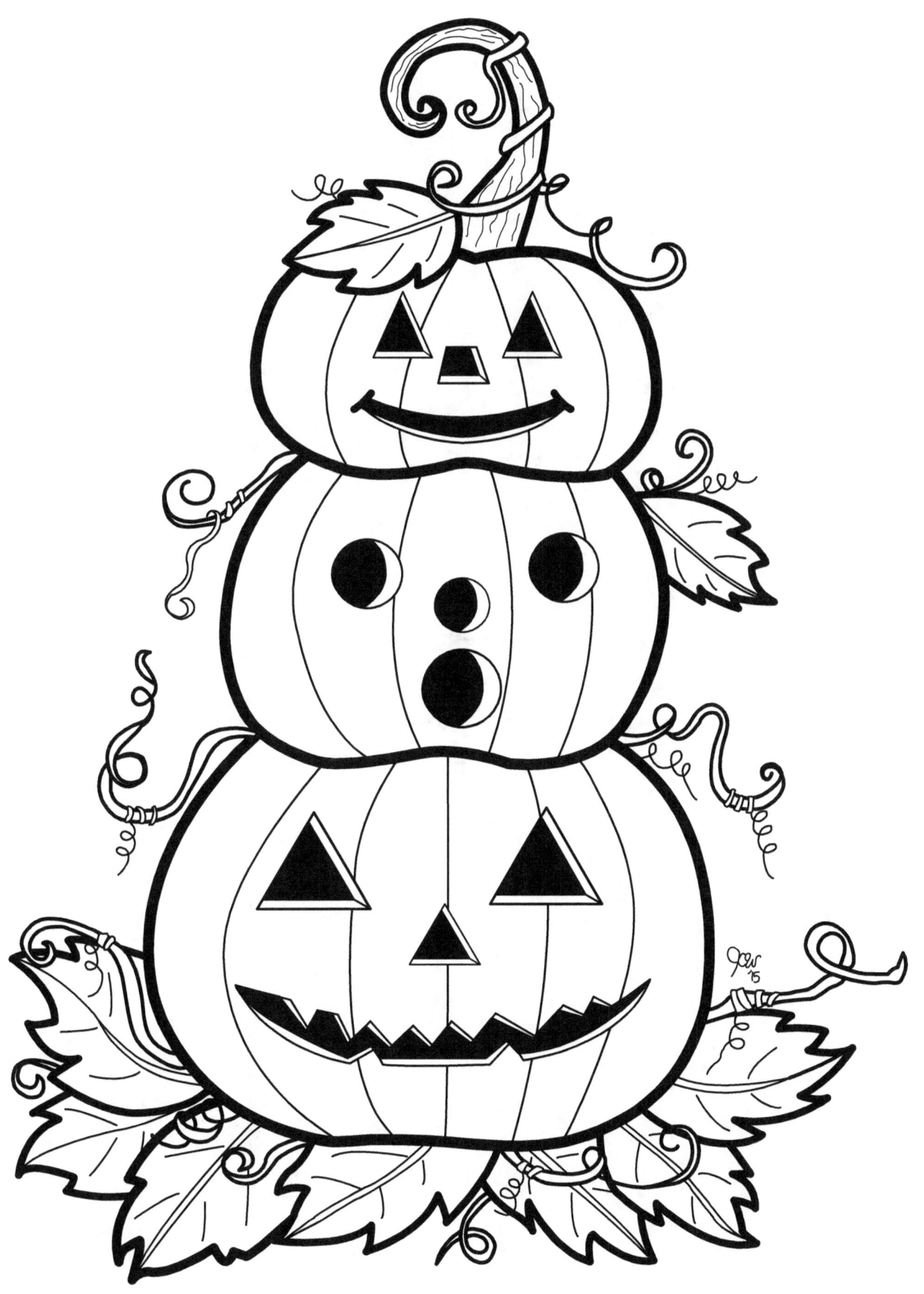

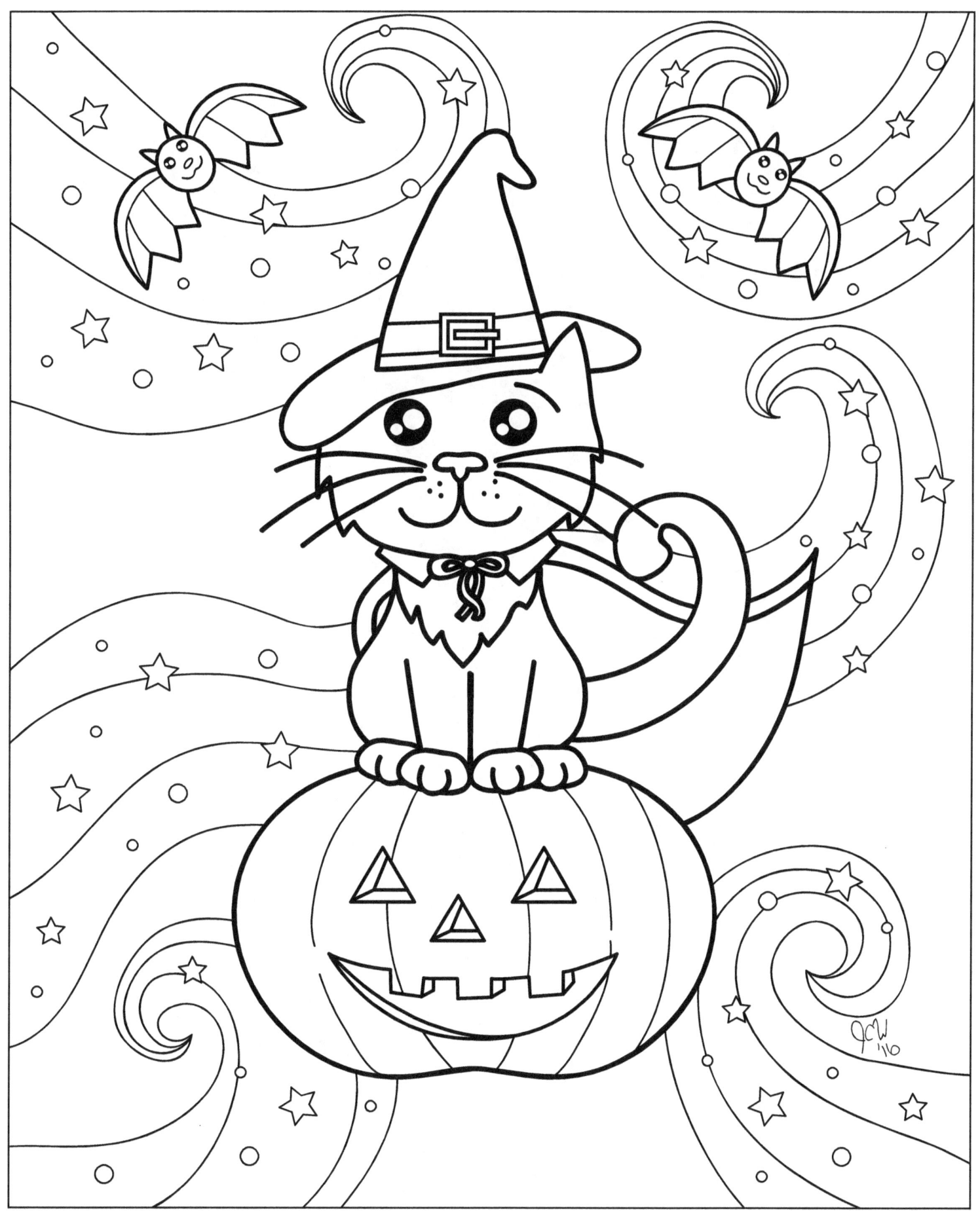

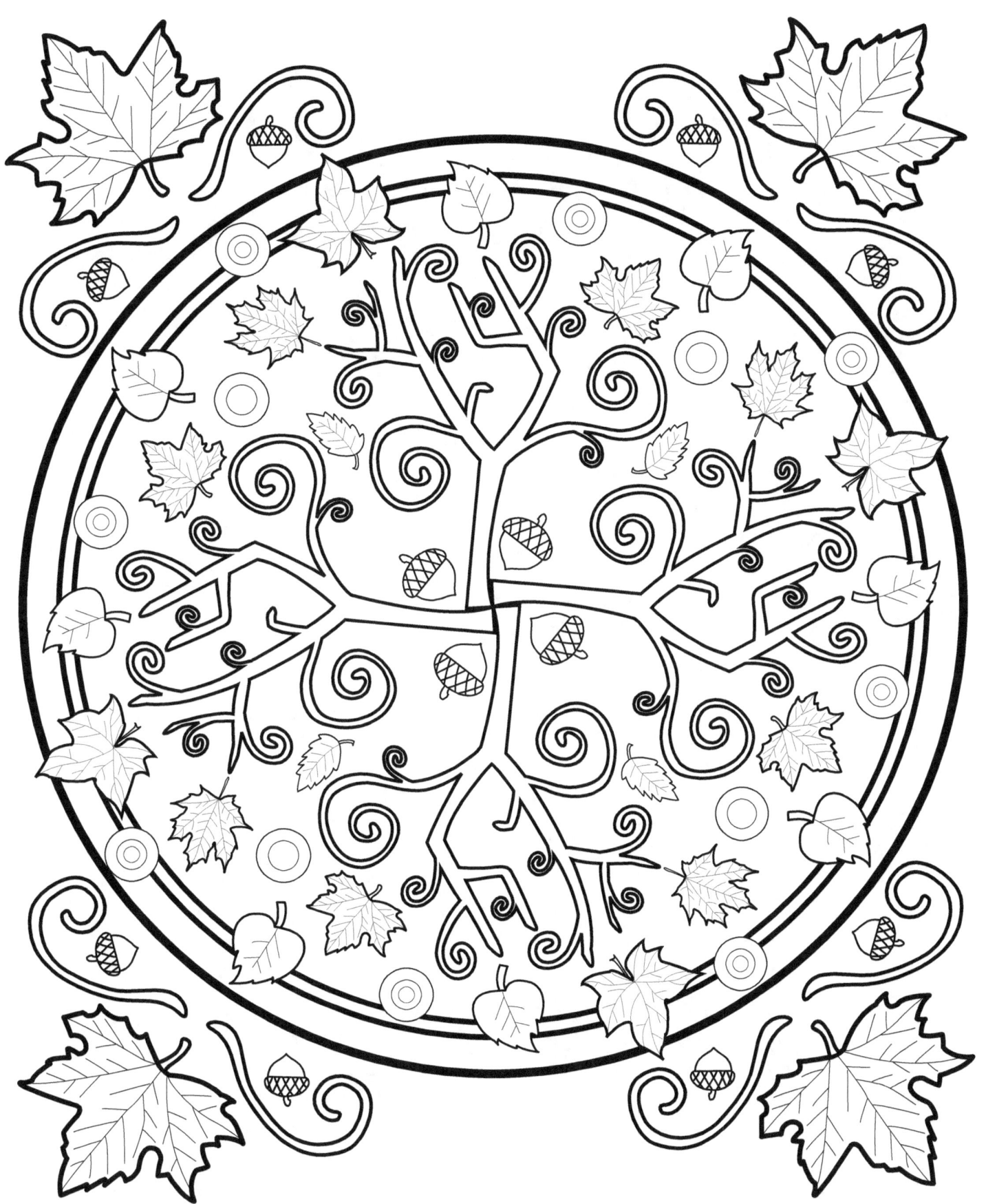

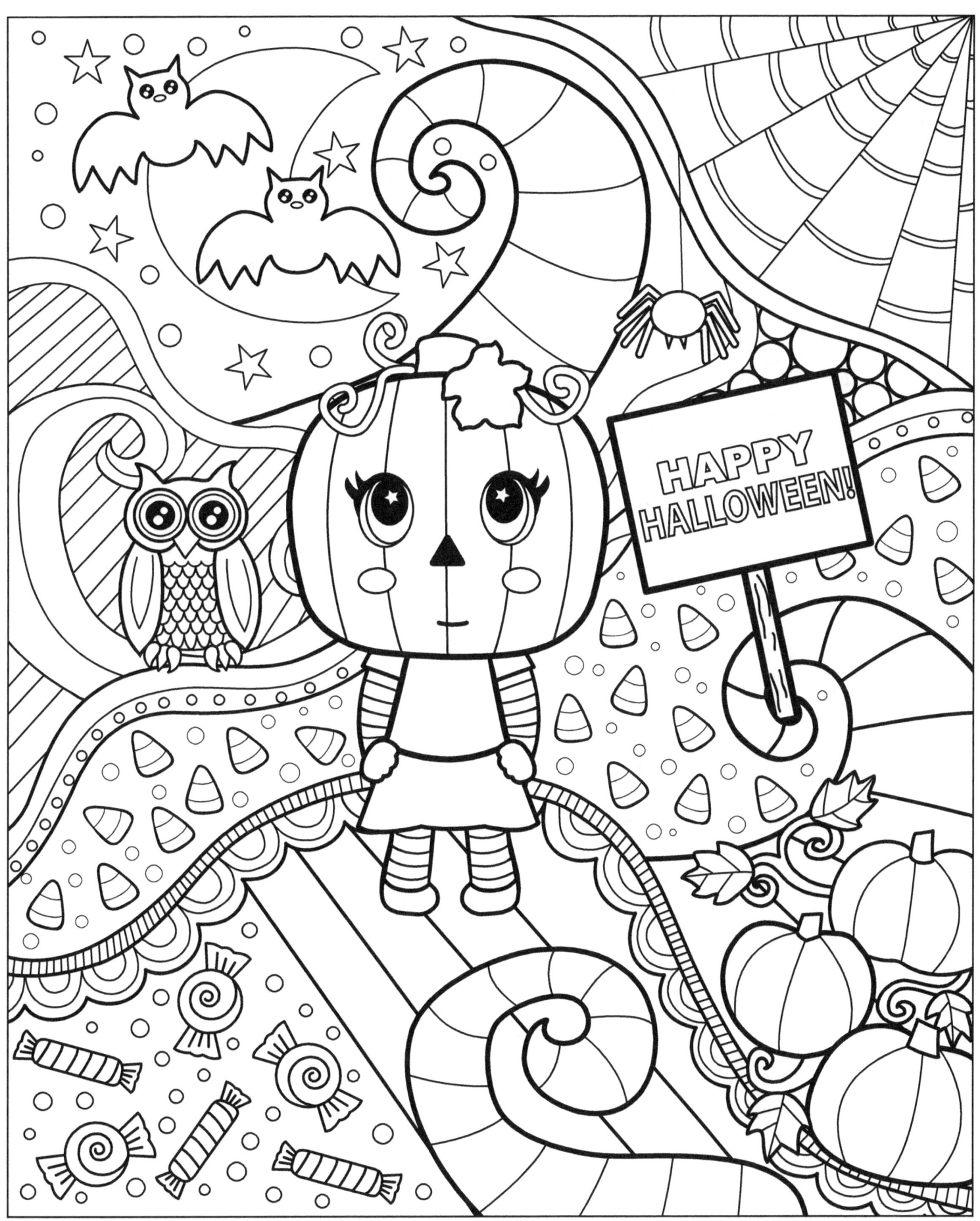

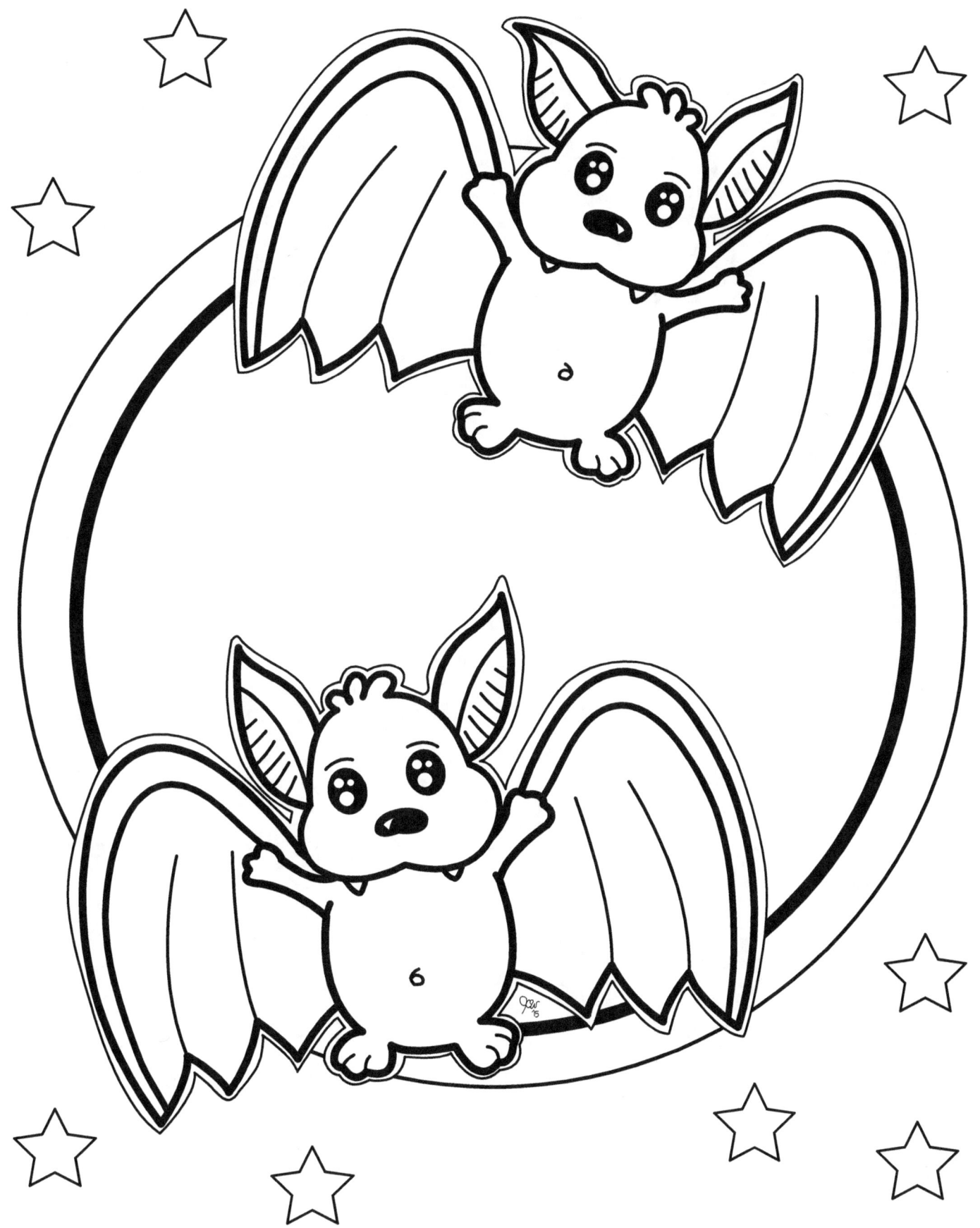

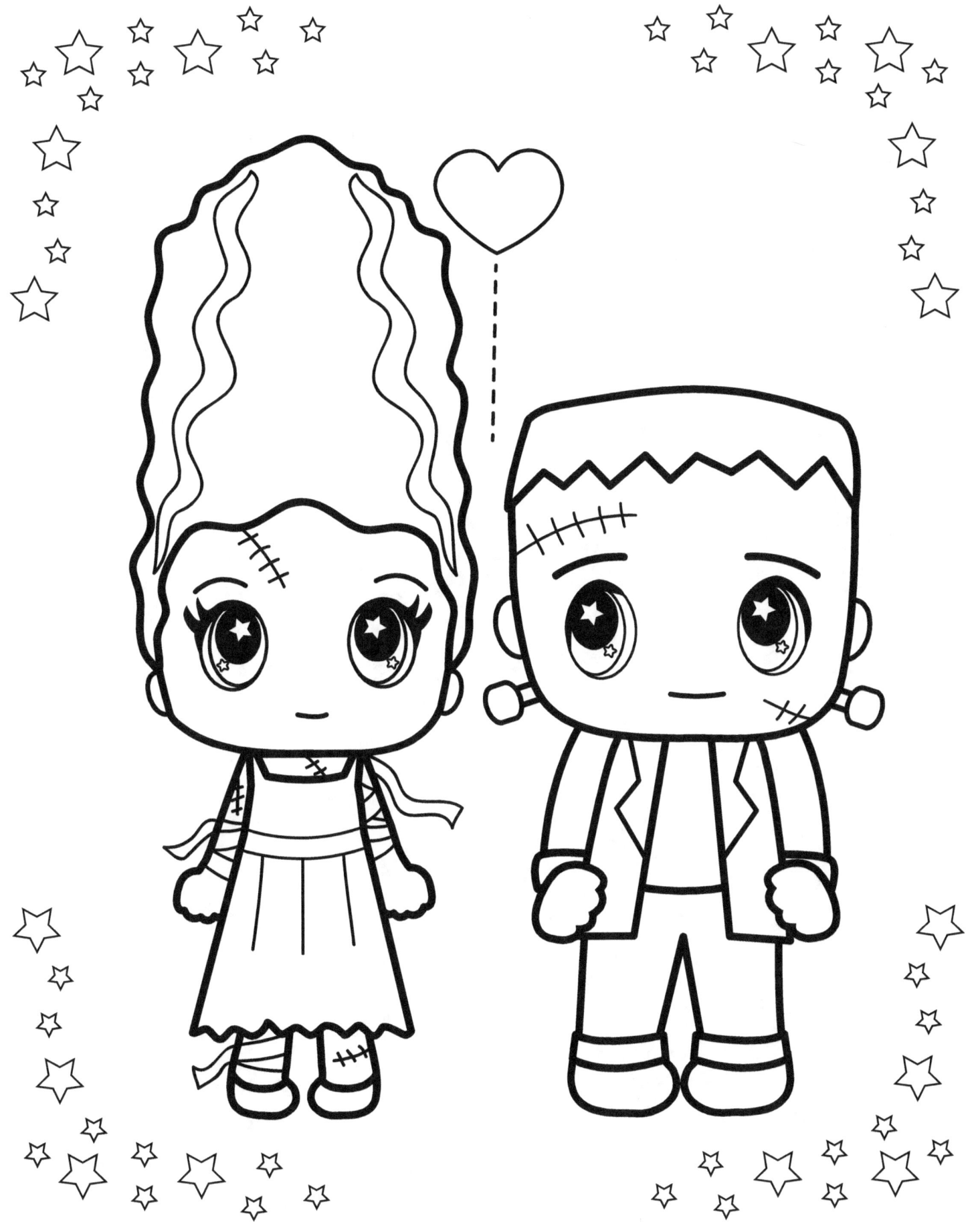

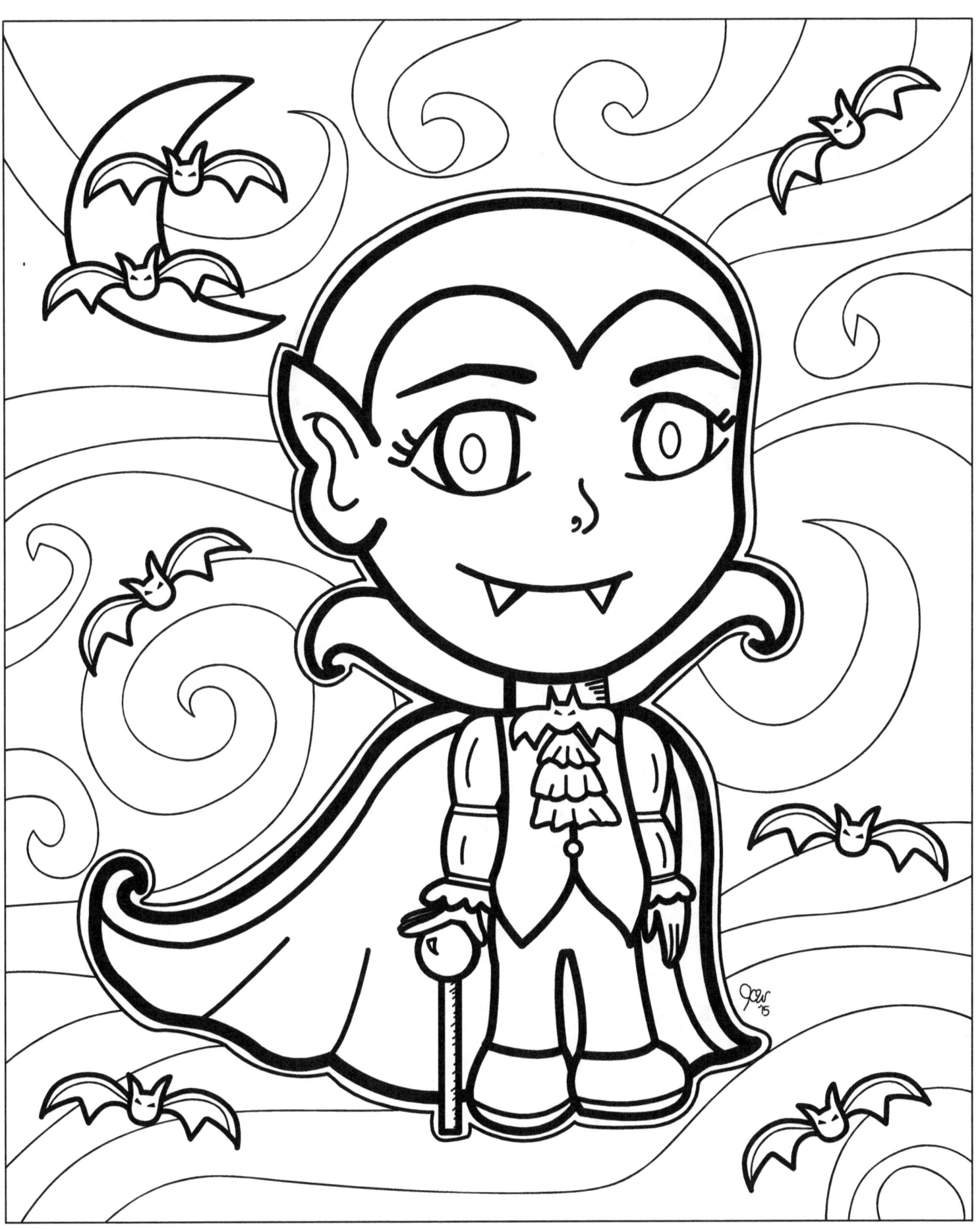

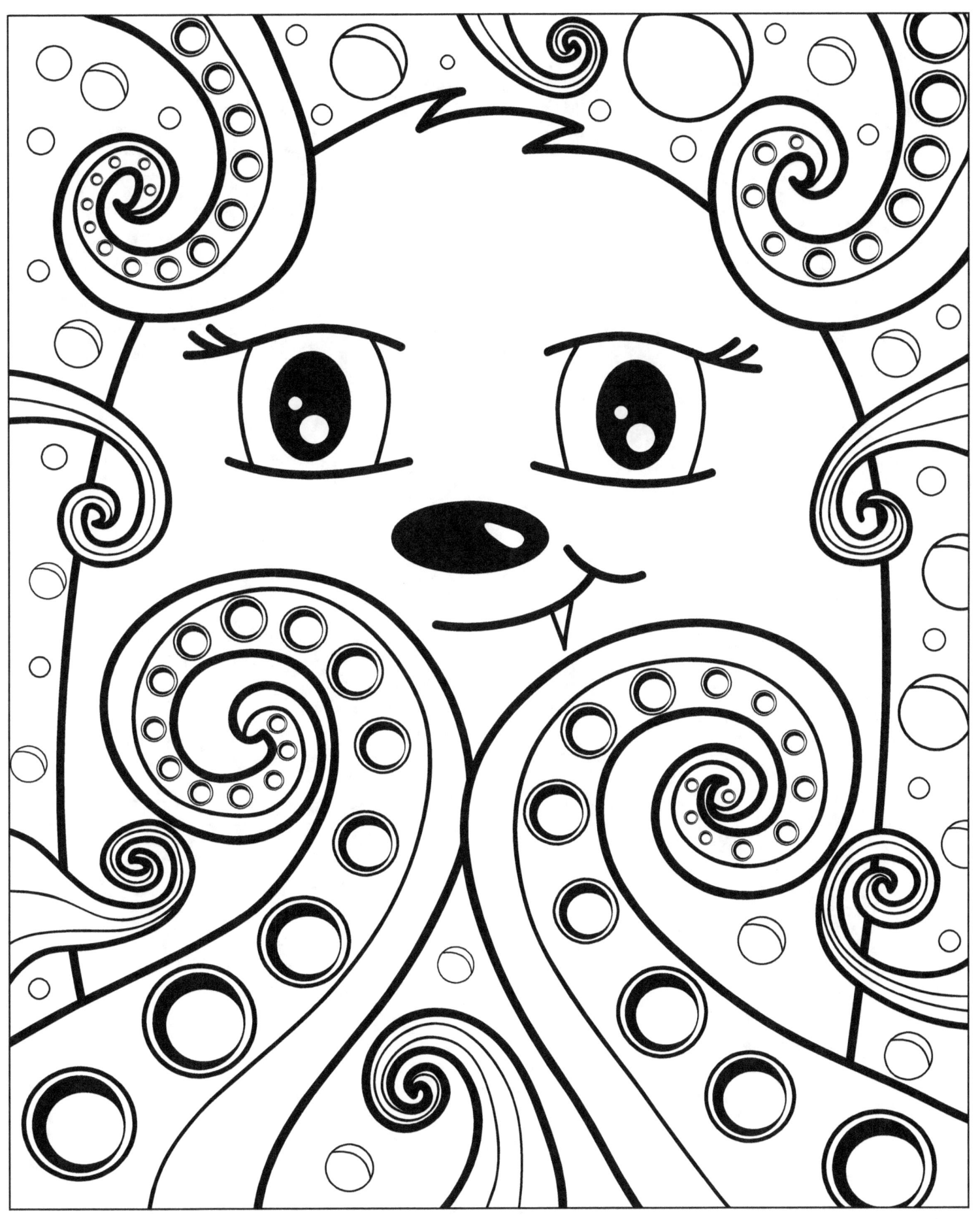

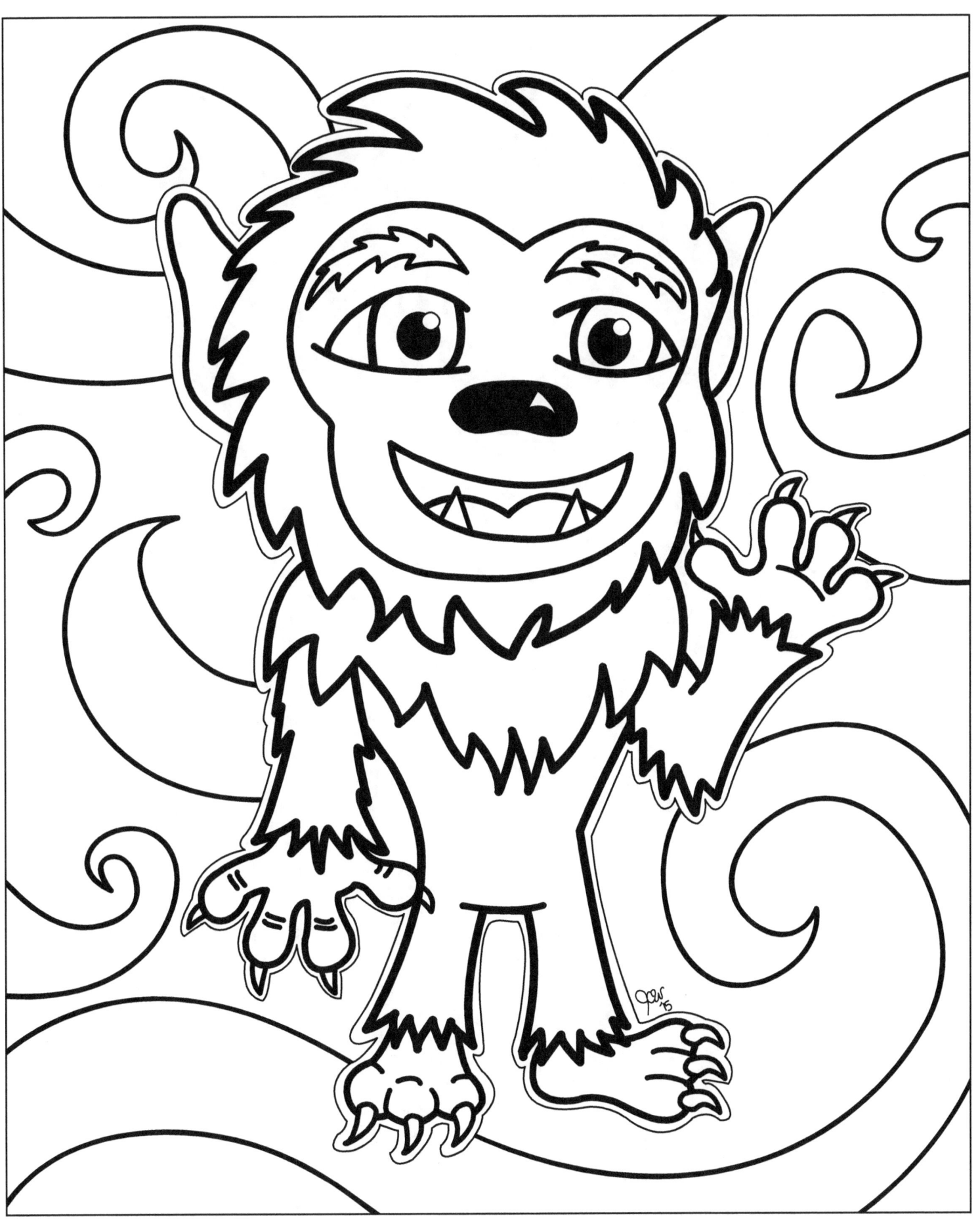

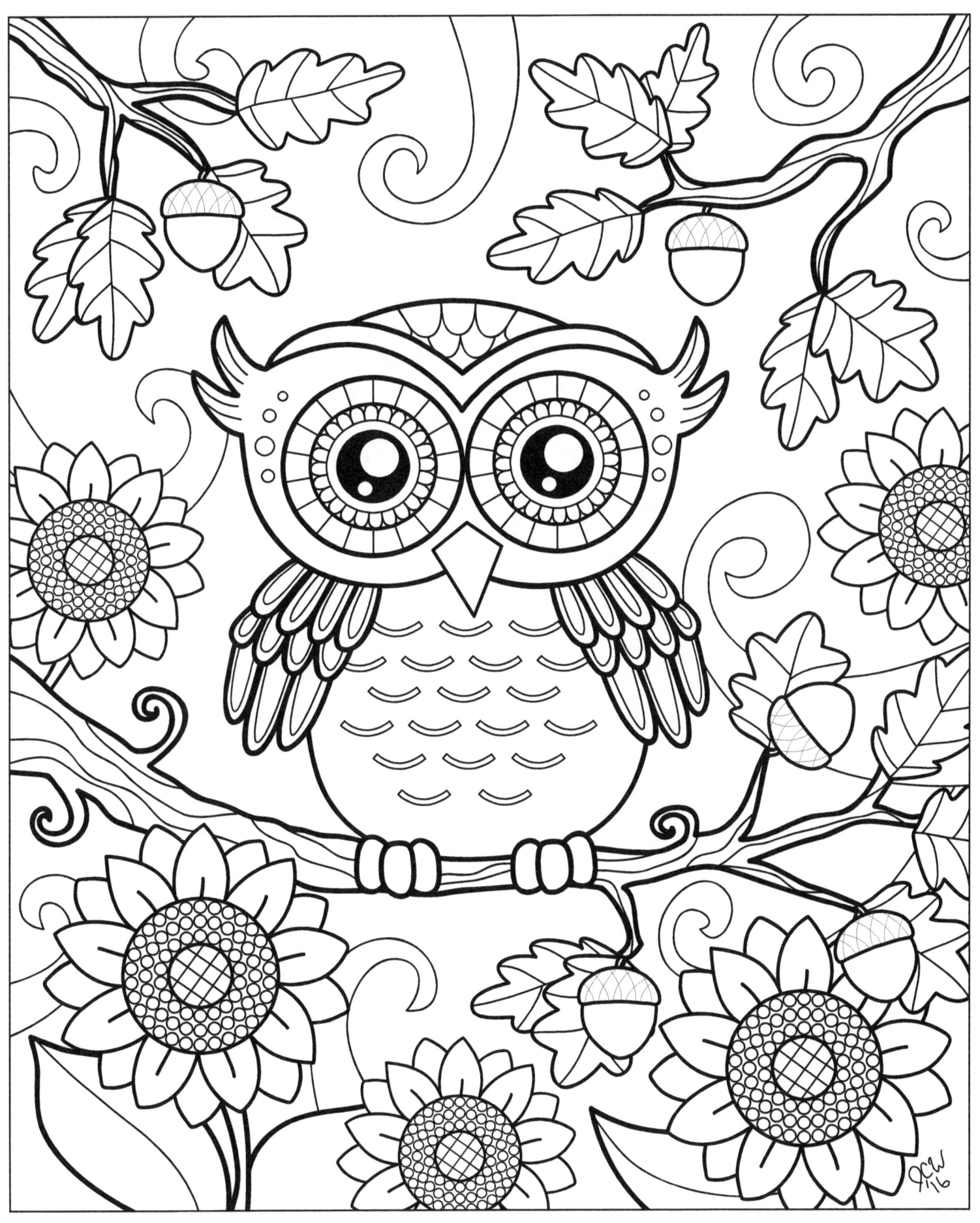

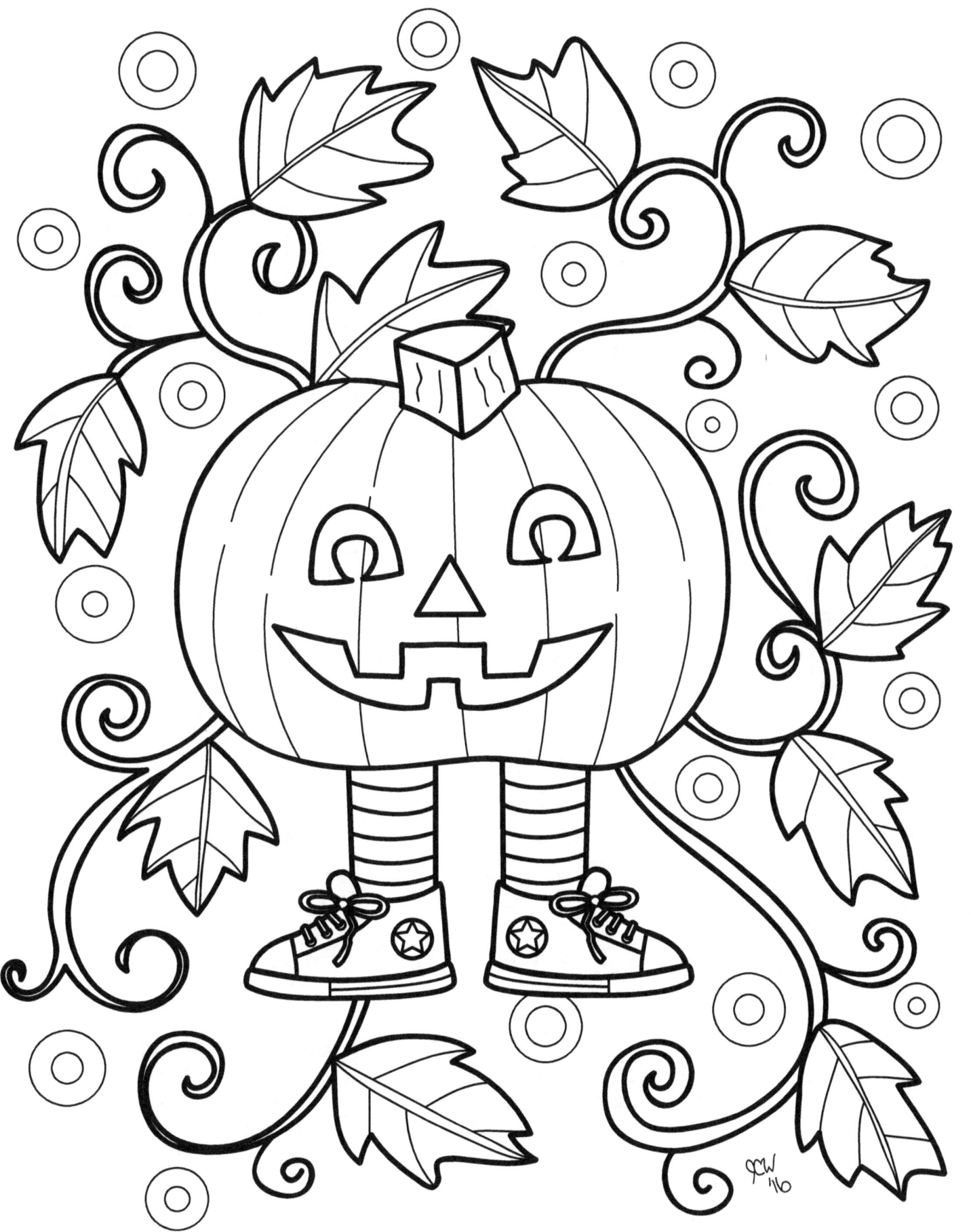

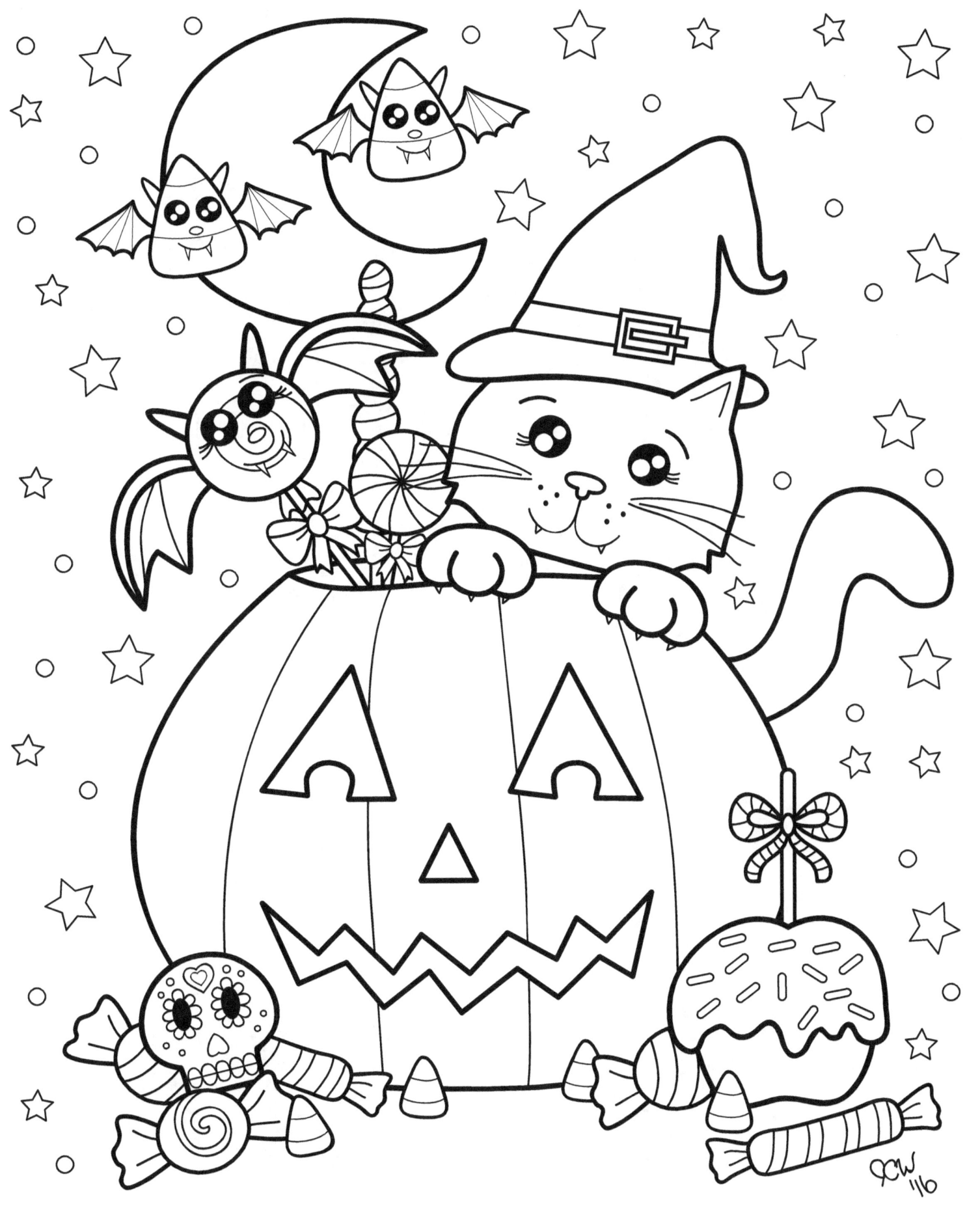

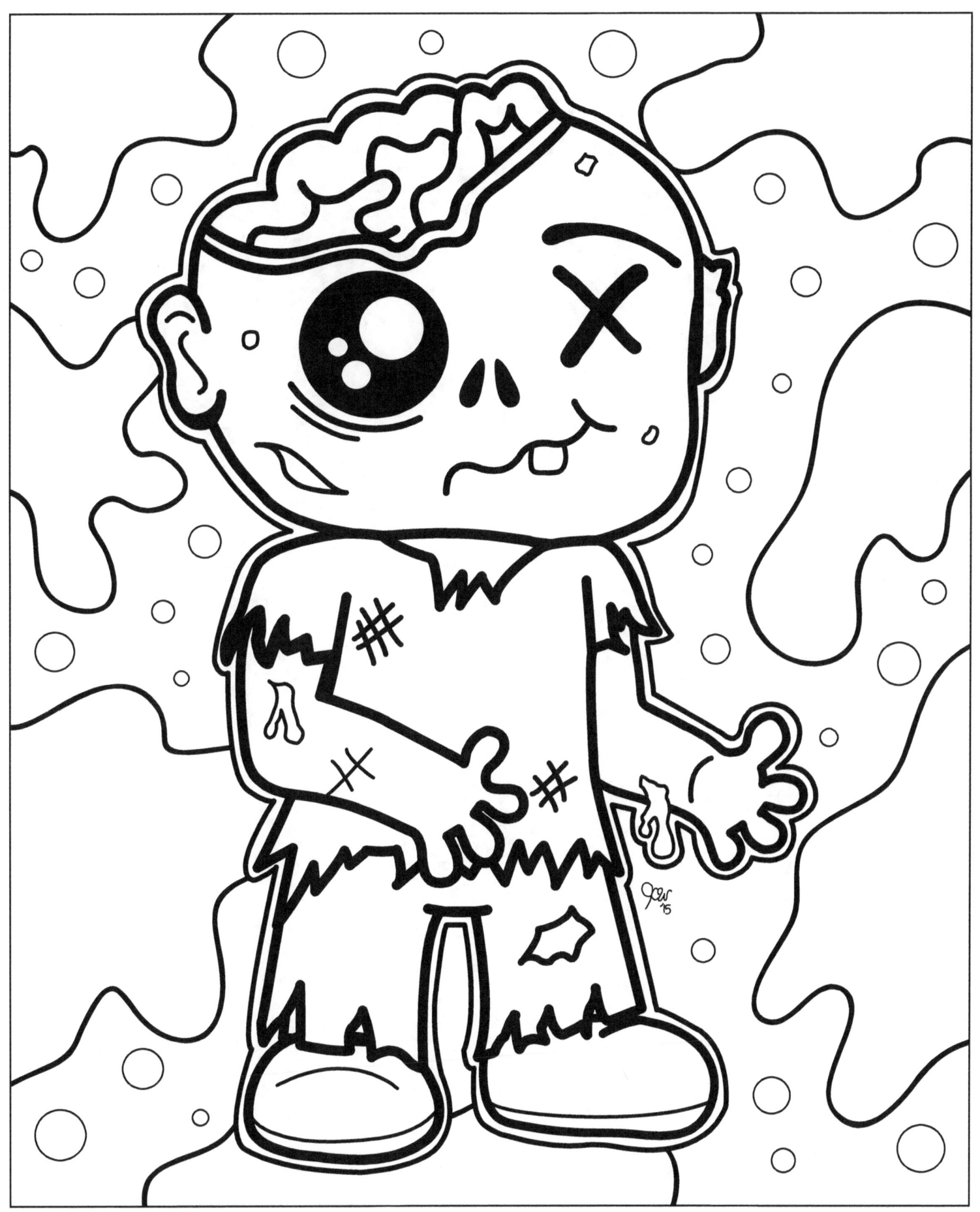

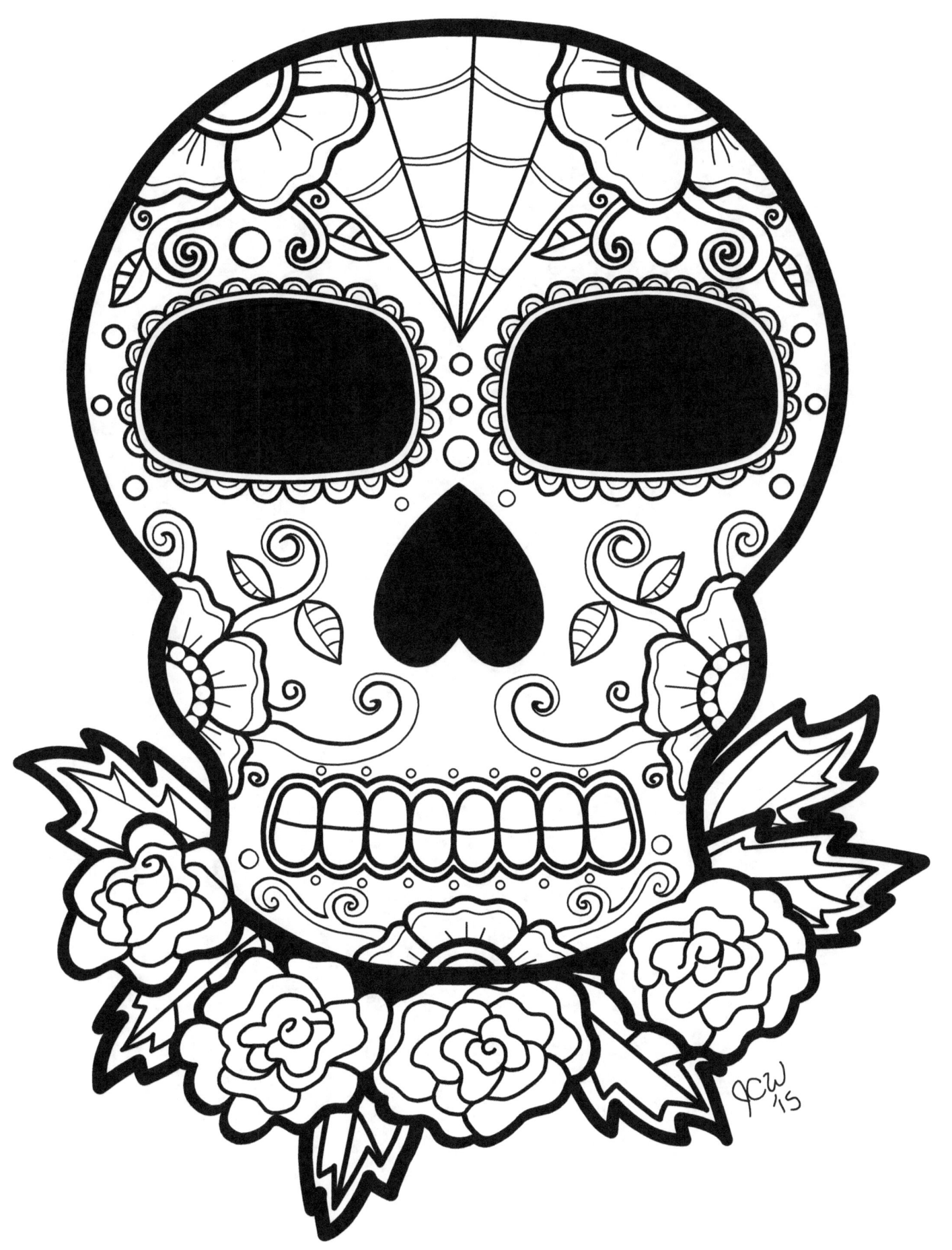

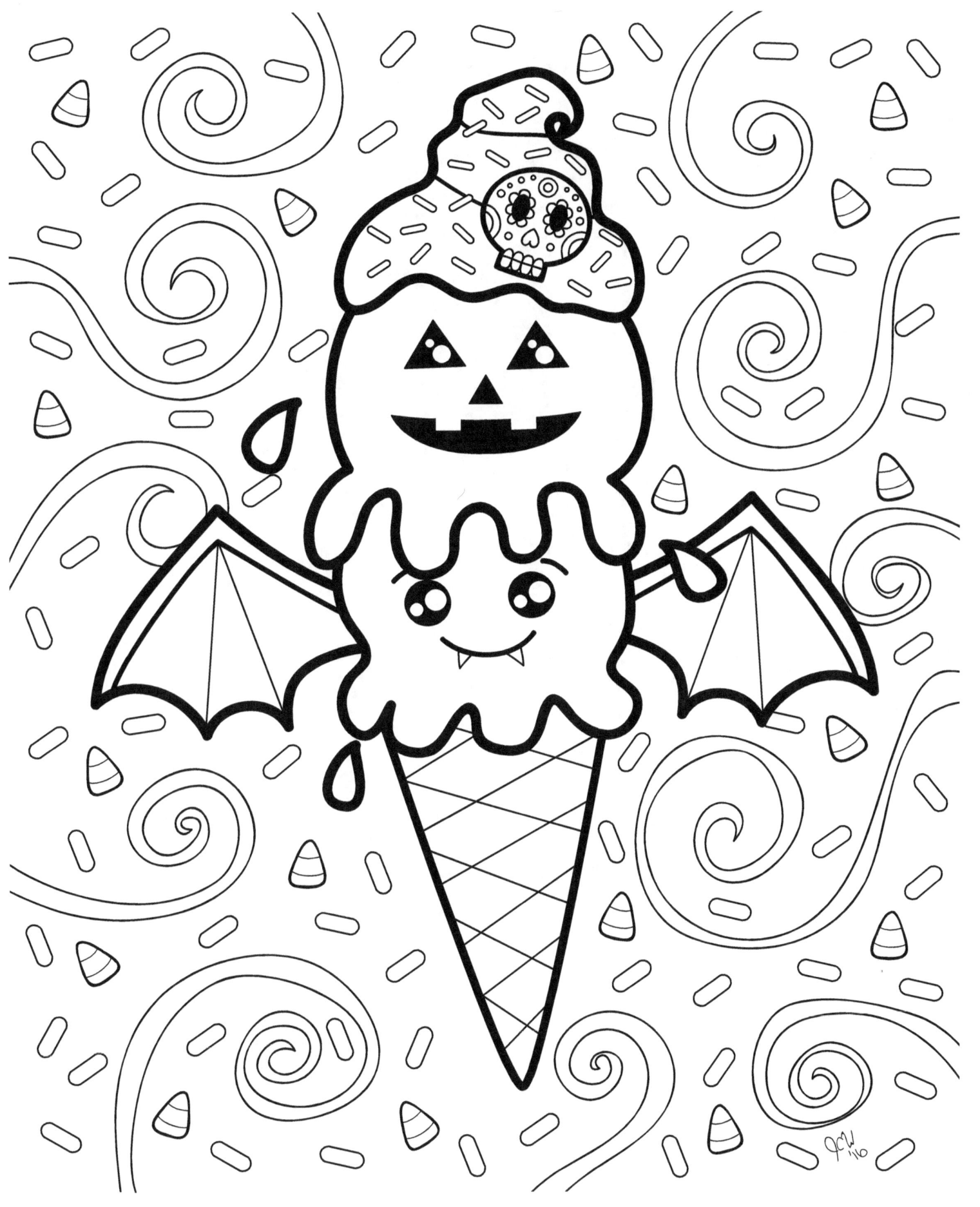

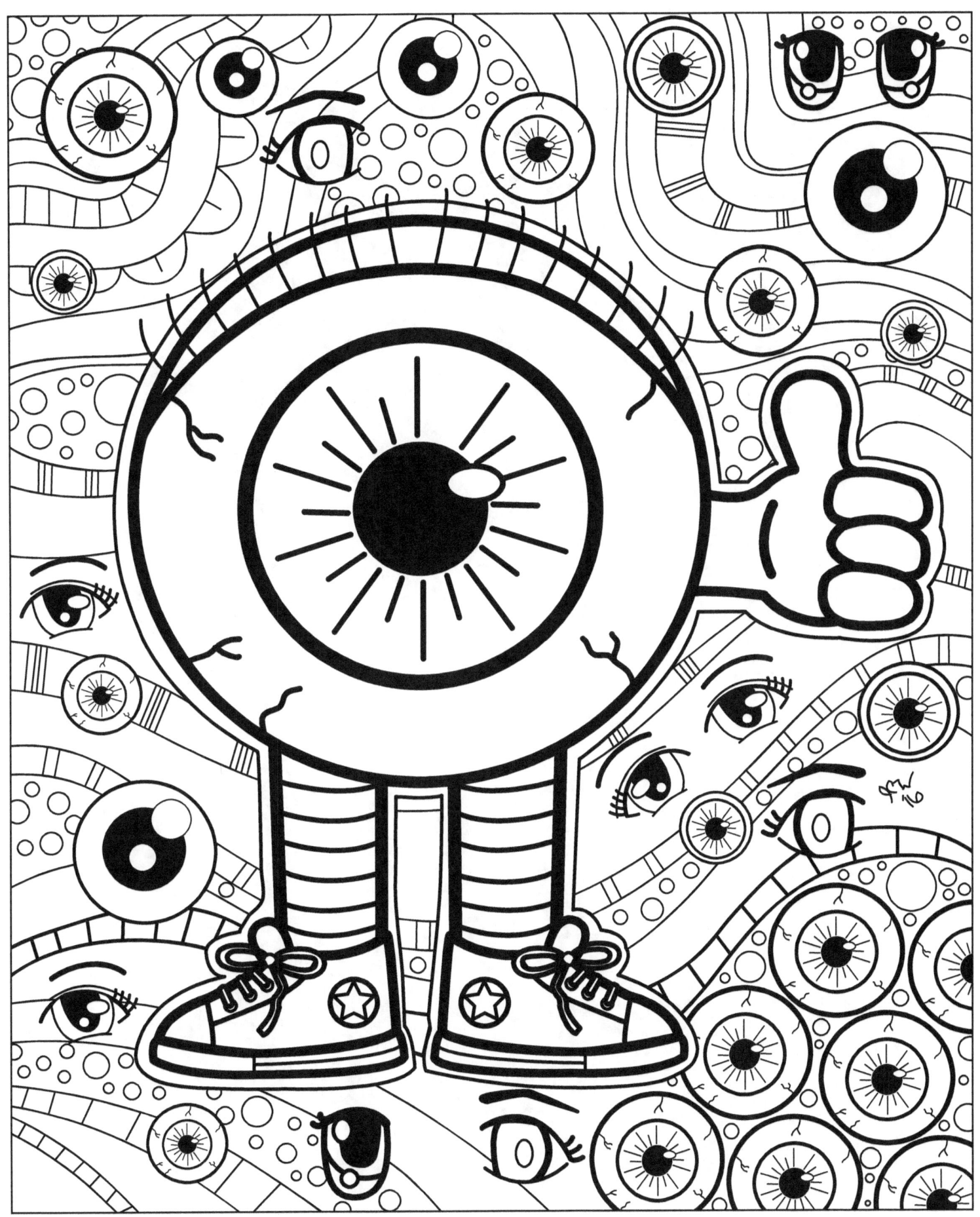

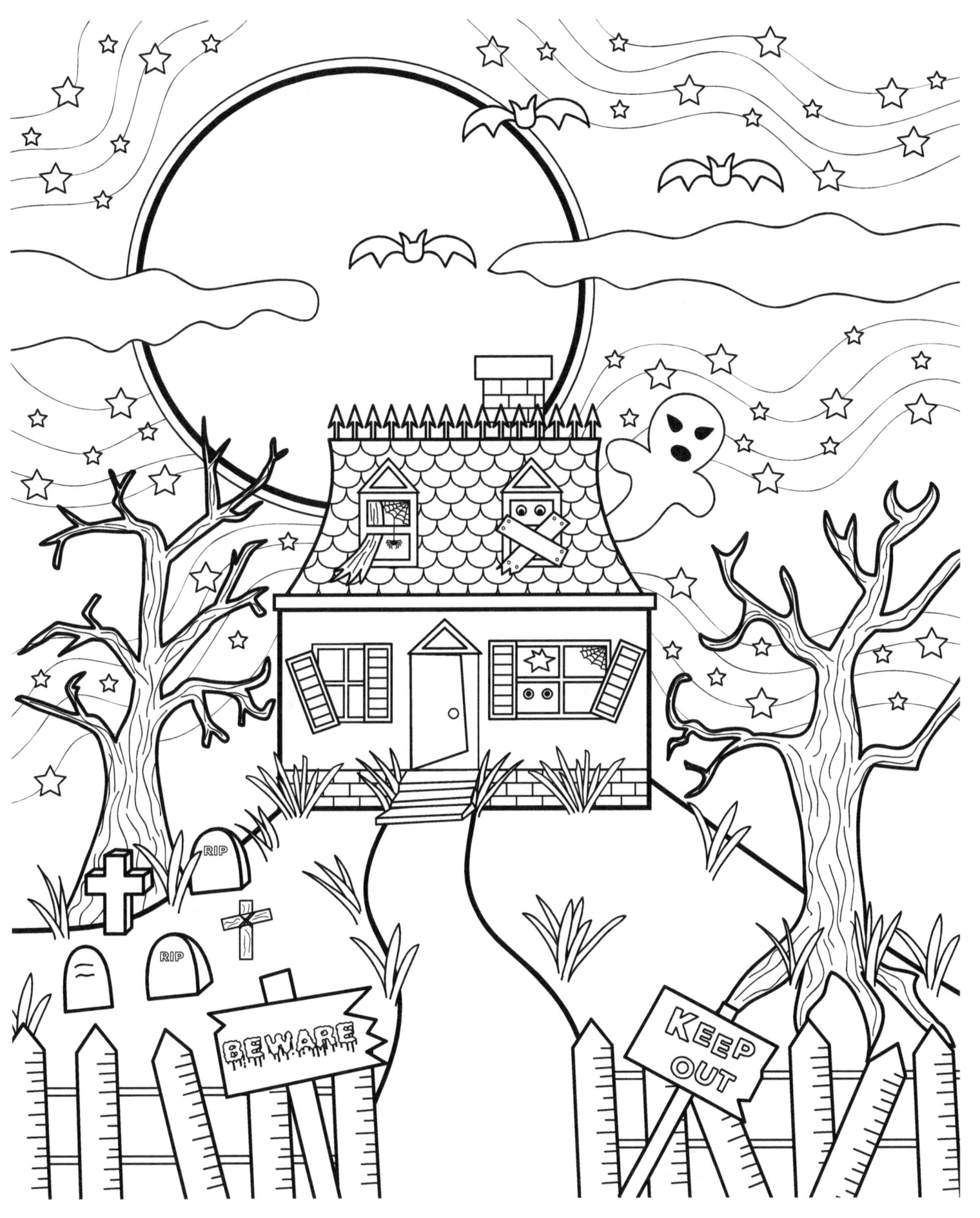

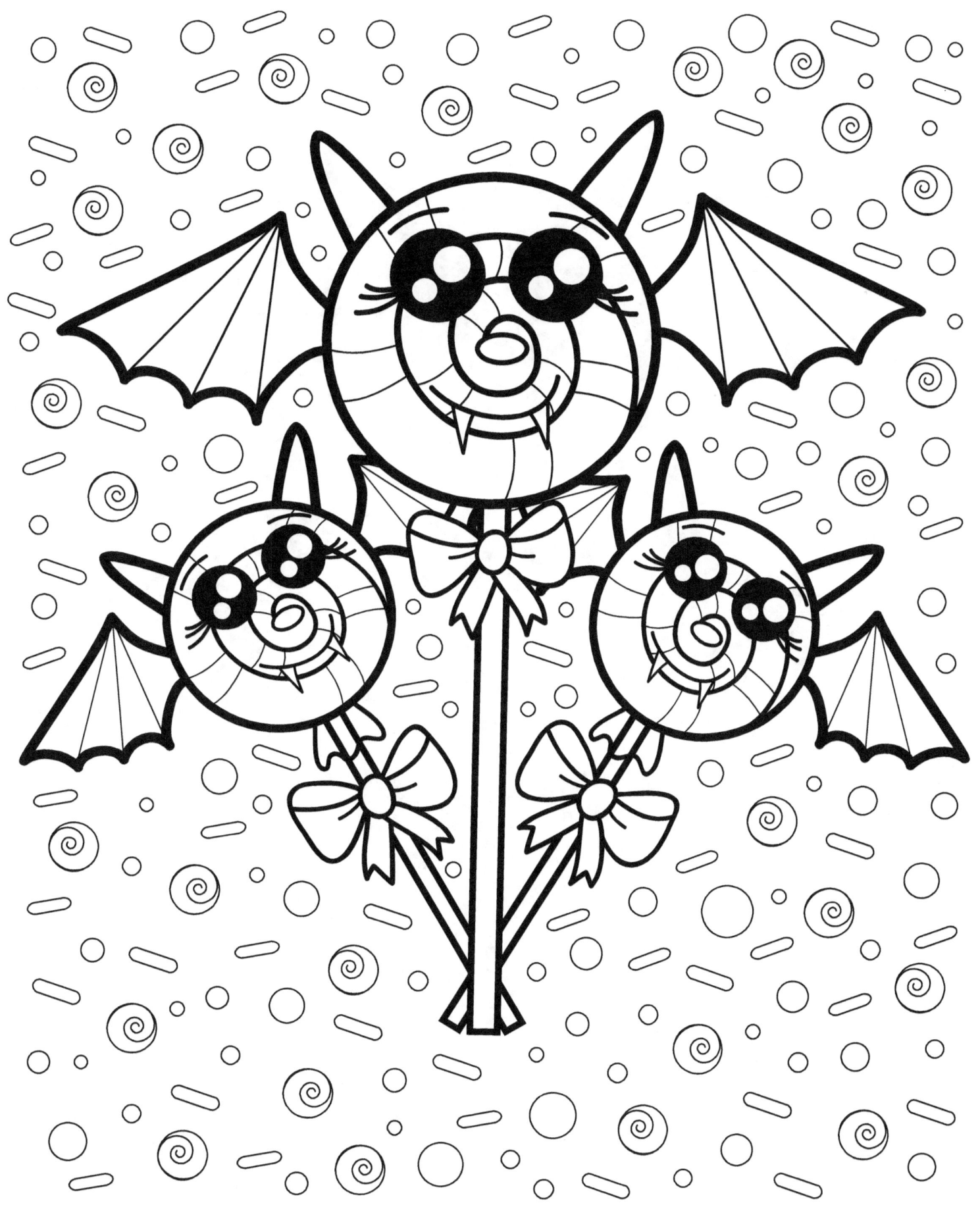

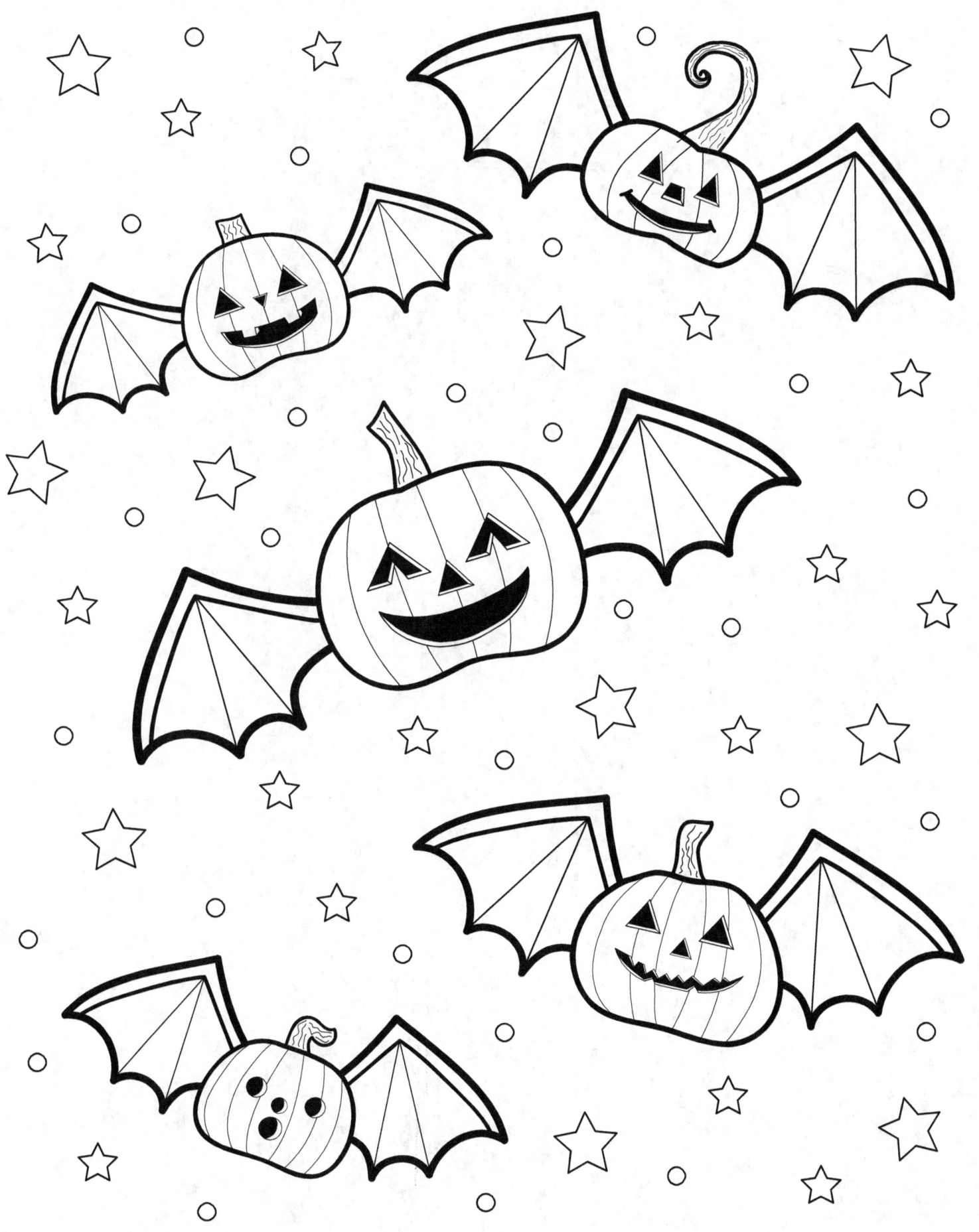

Bonus Pages

The following pages are some of the previous designs, but done in midnight style printed on black pages for your enjoyment.

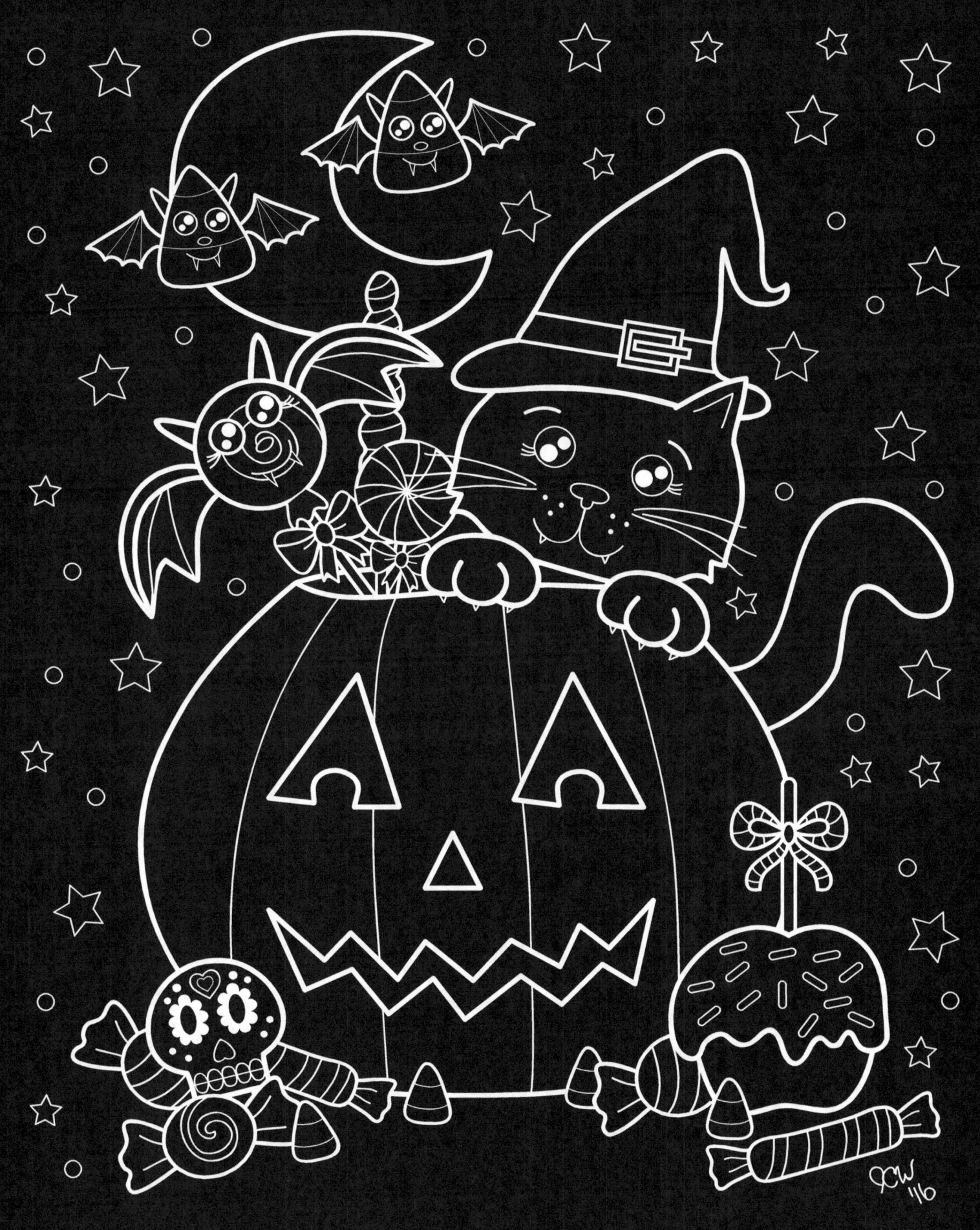

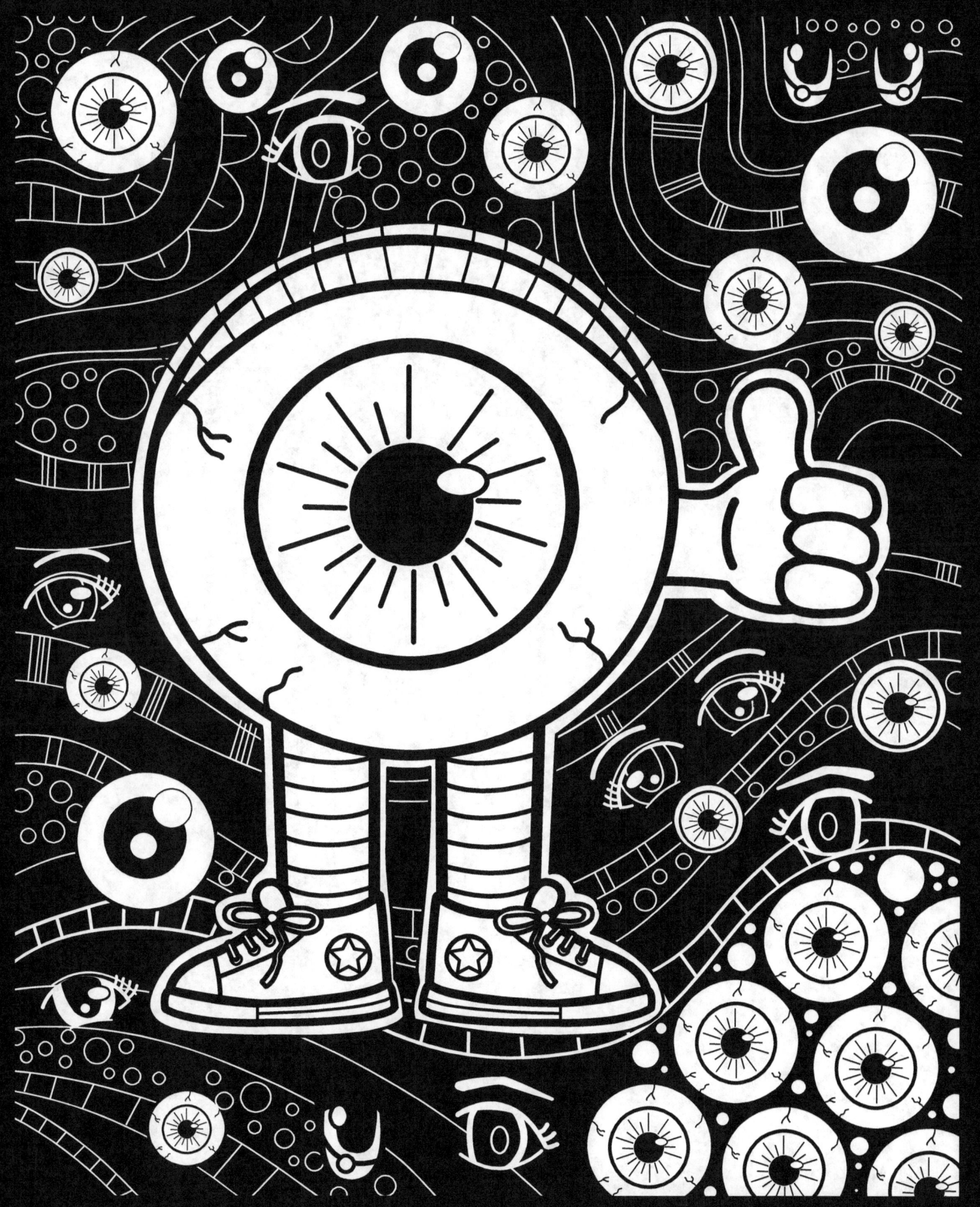

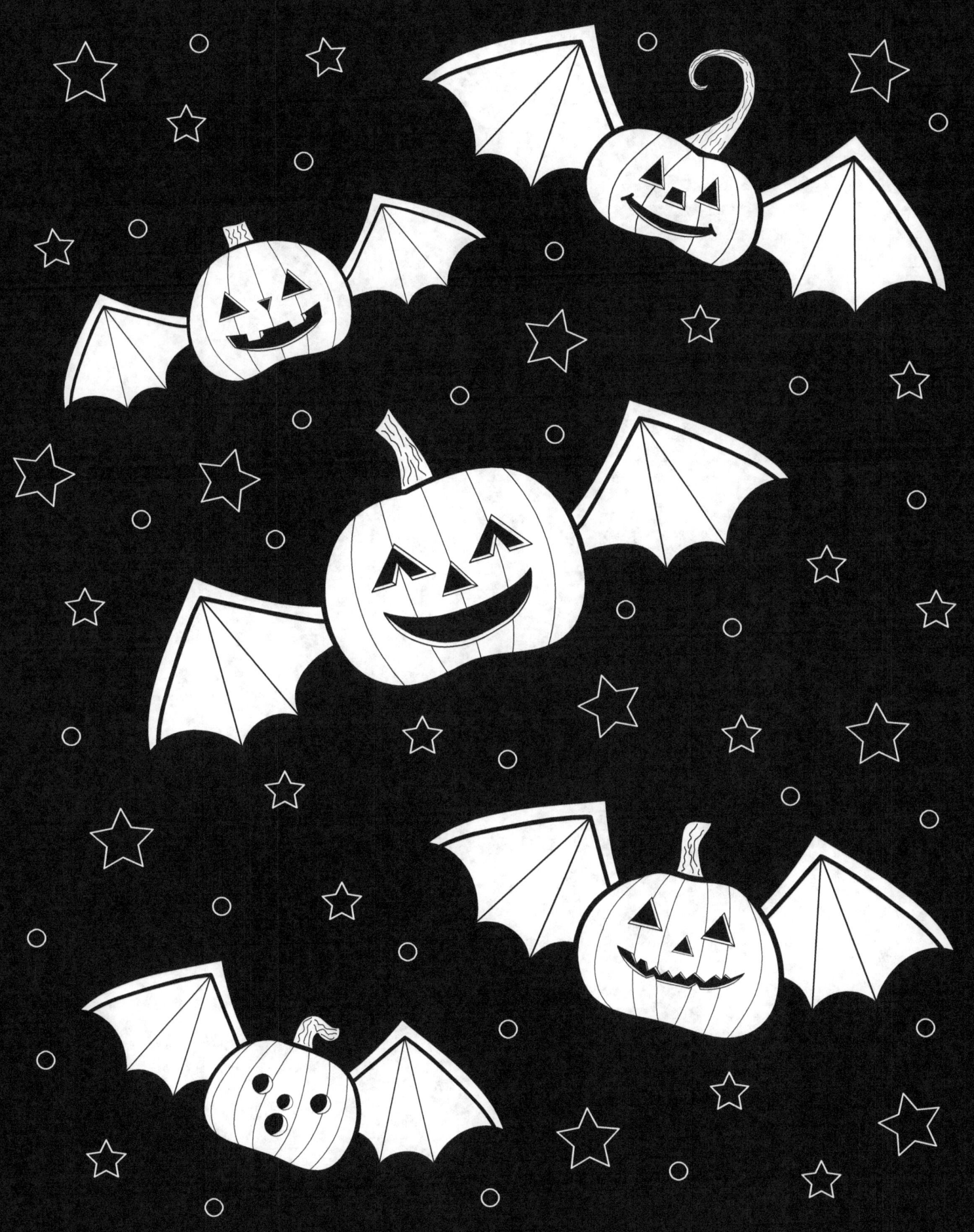

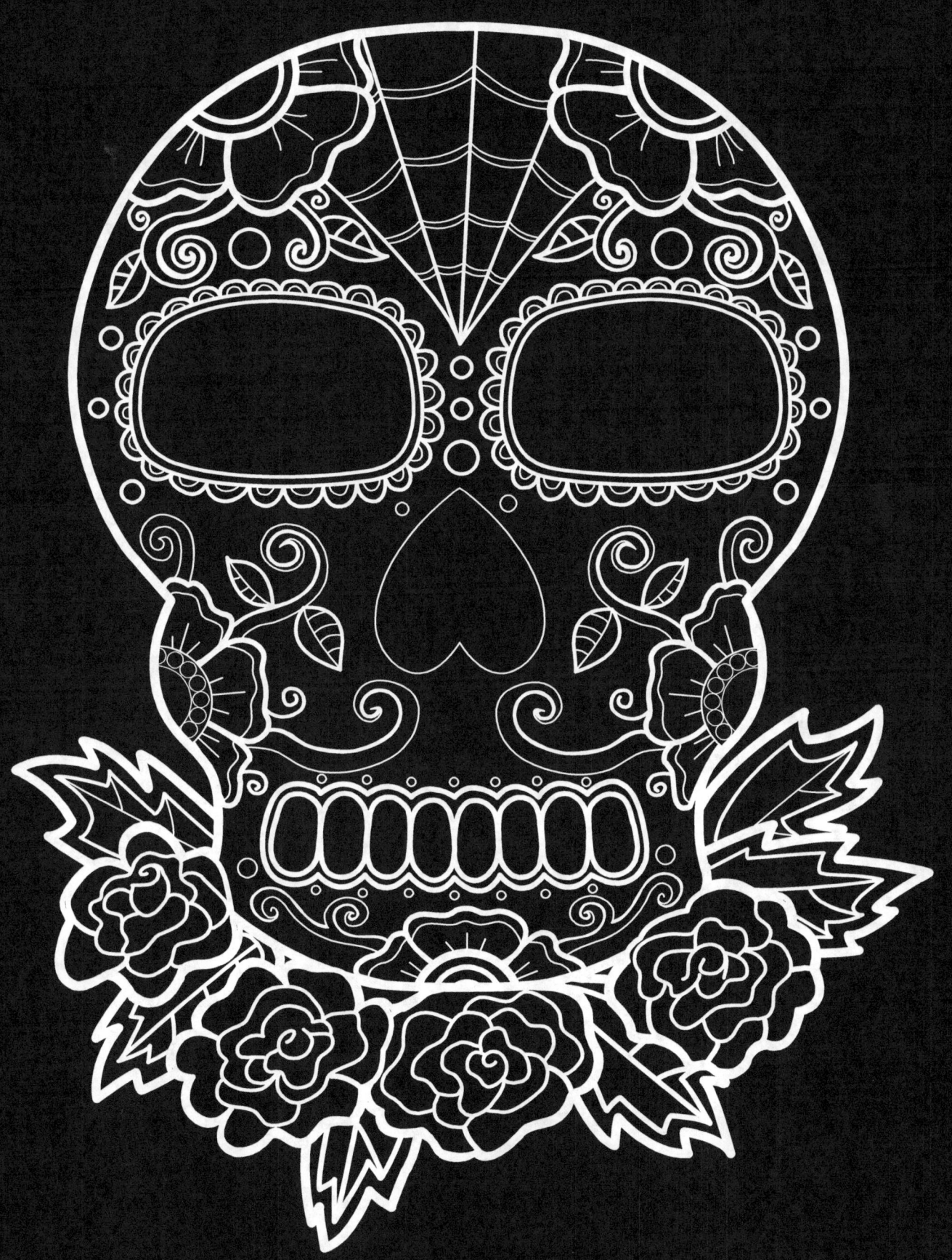

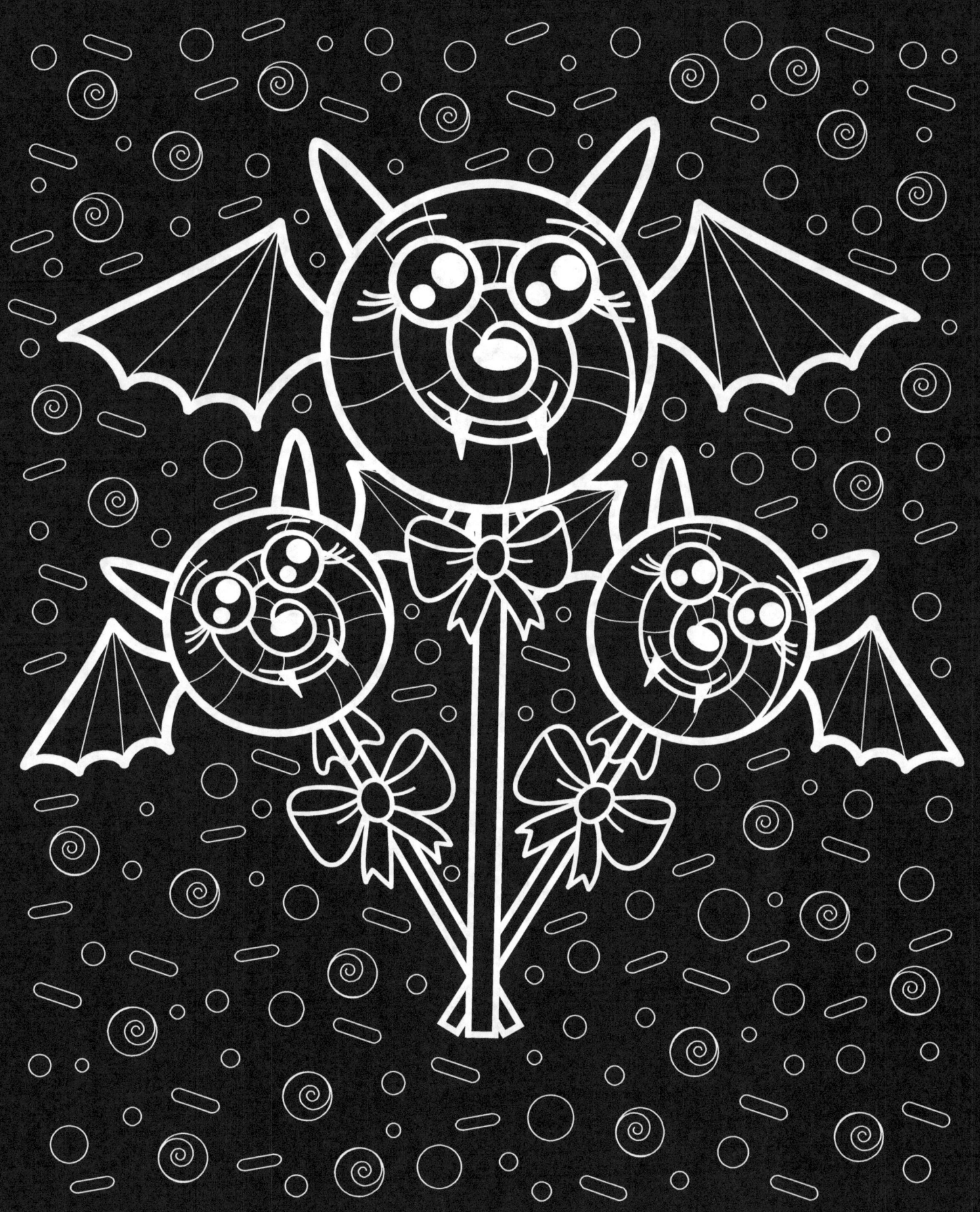

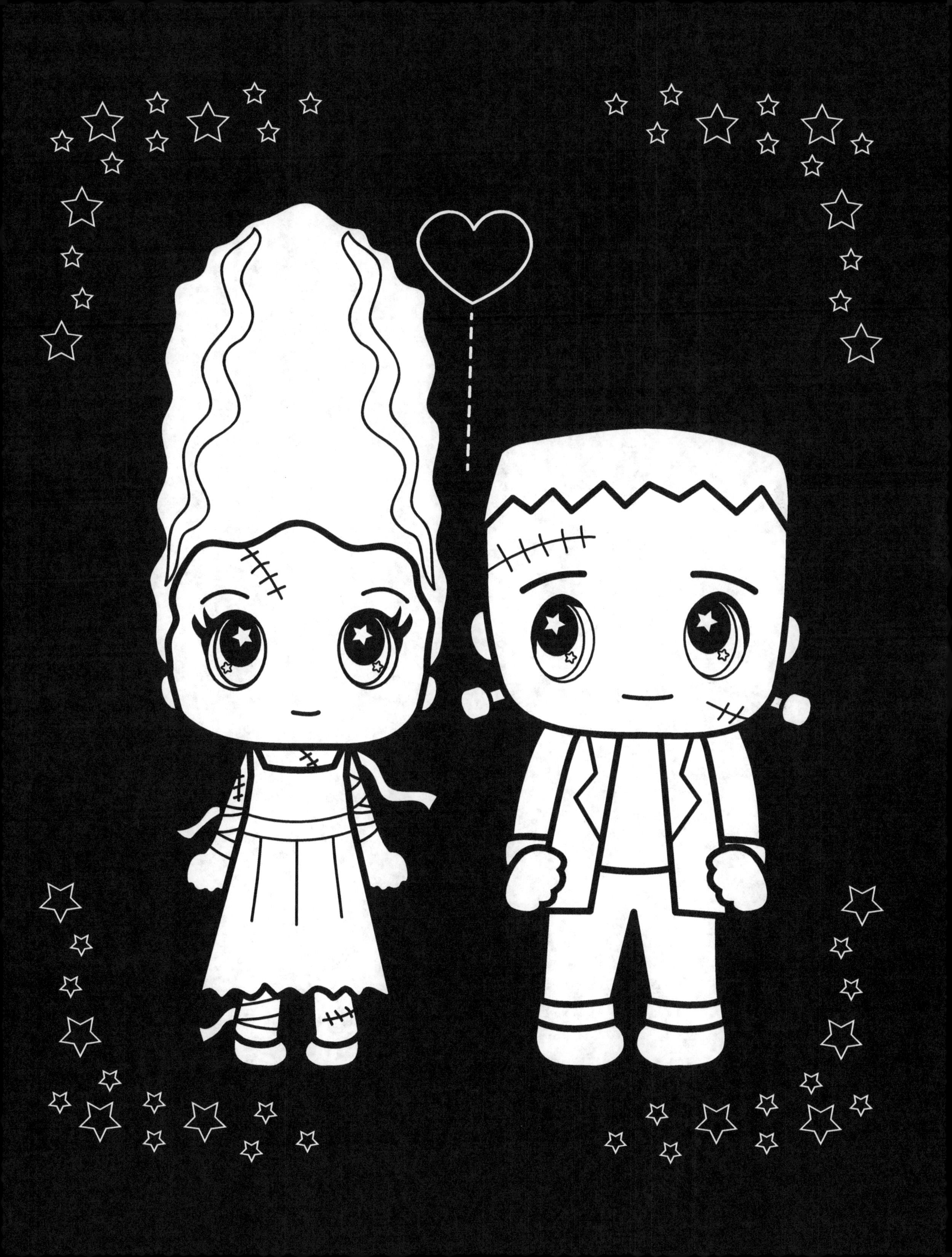

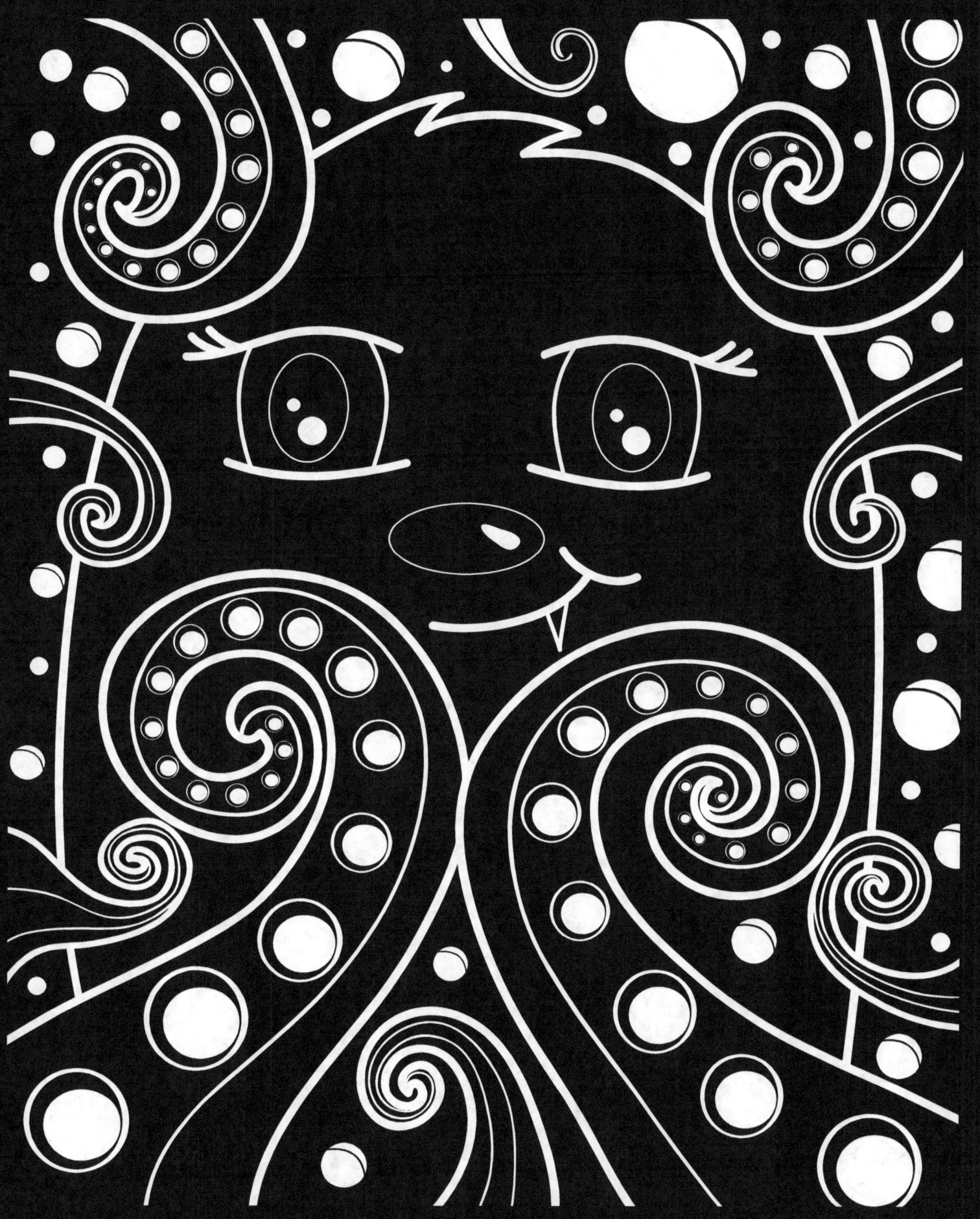

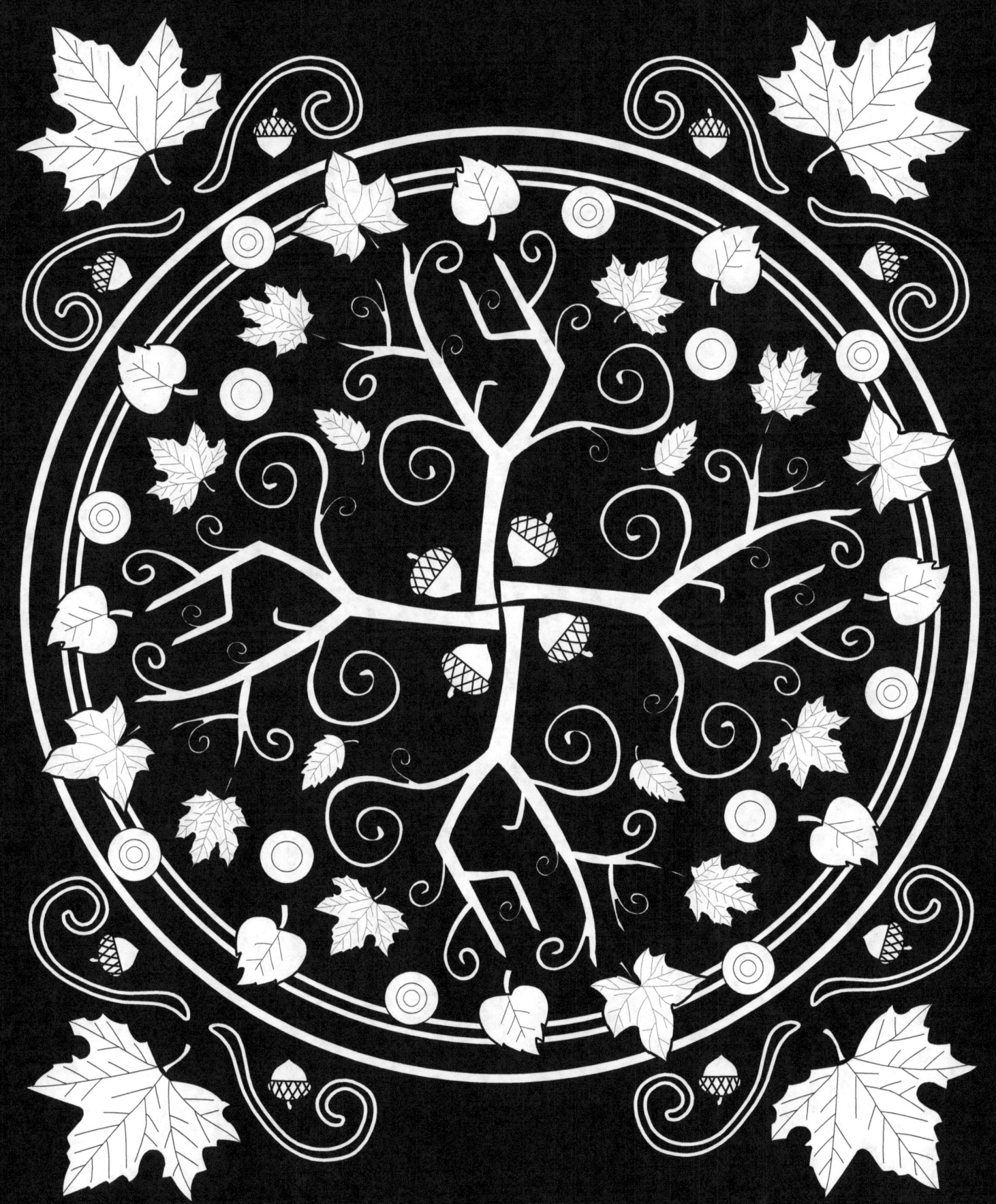

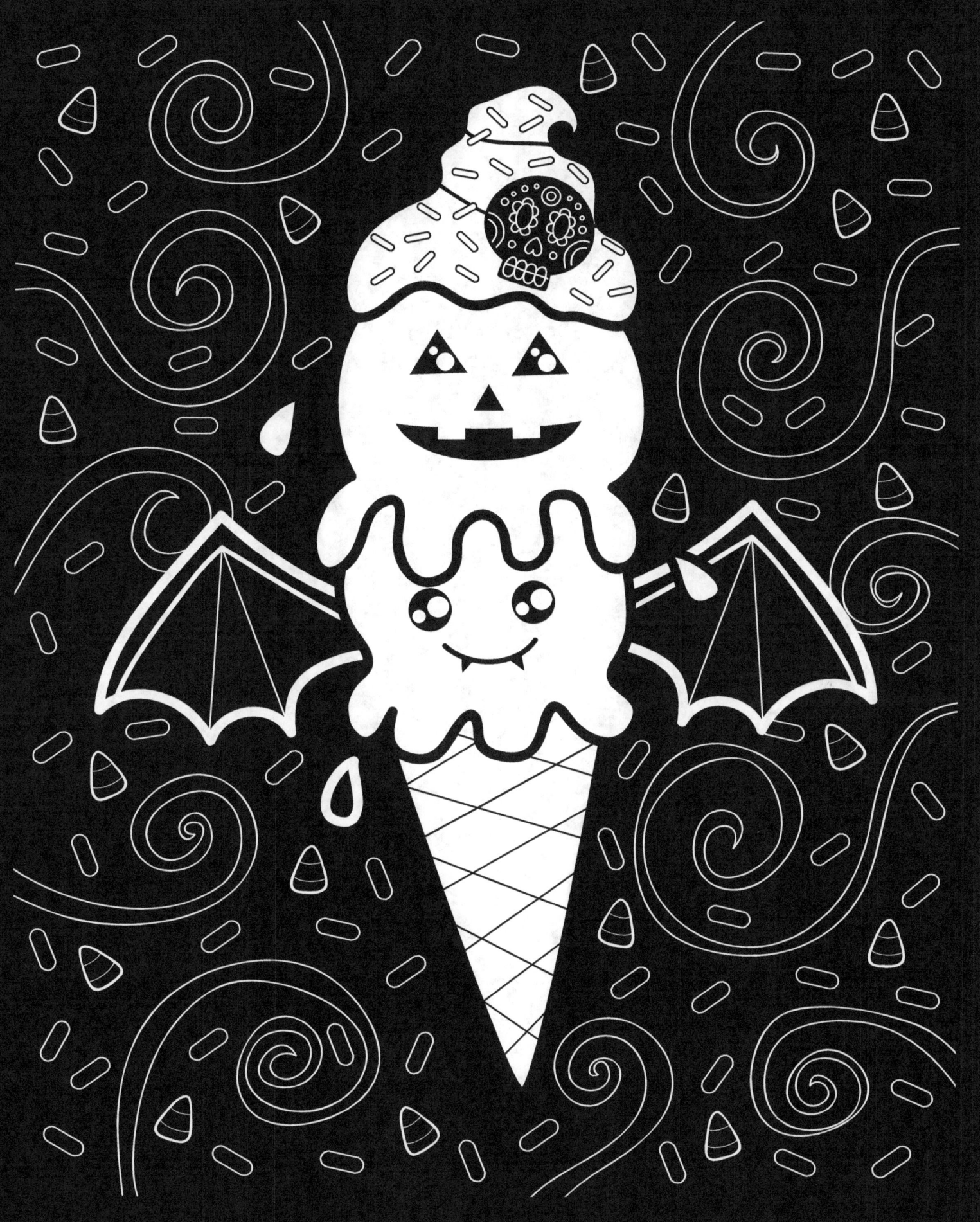

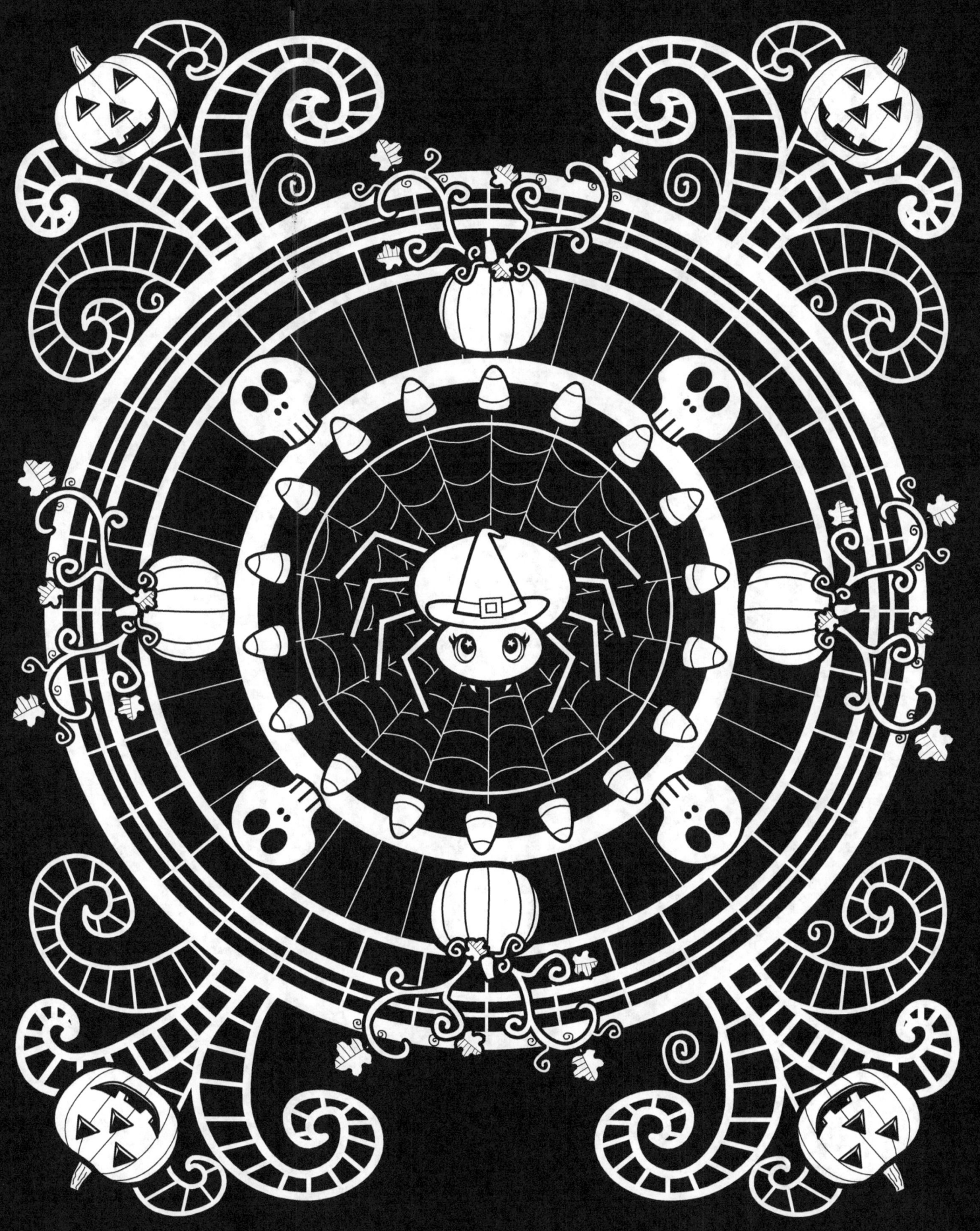

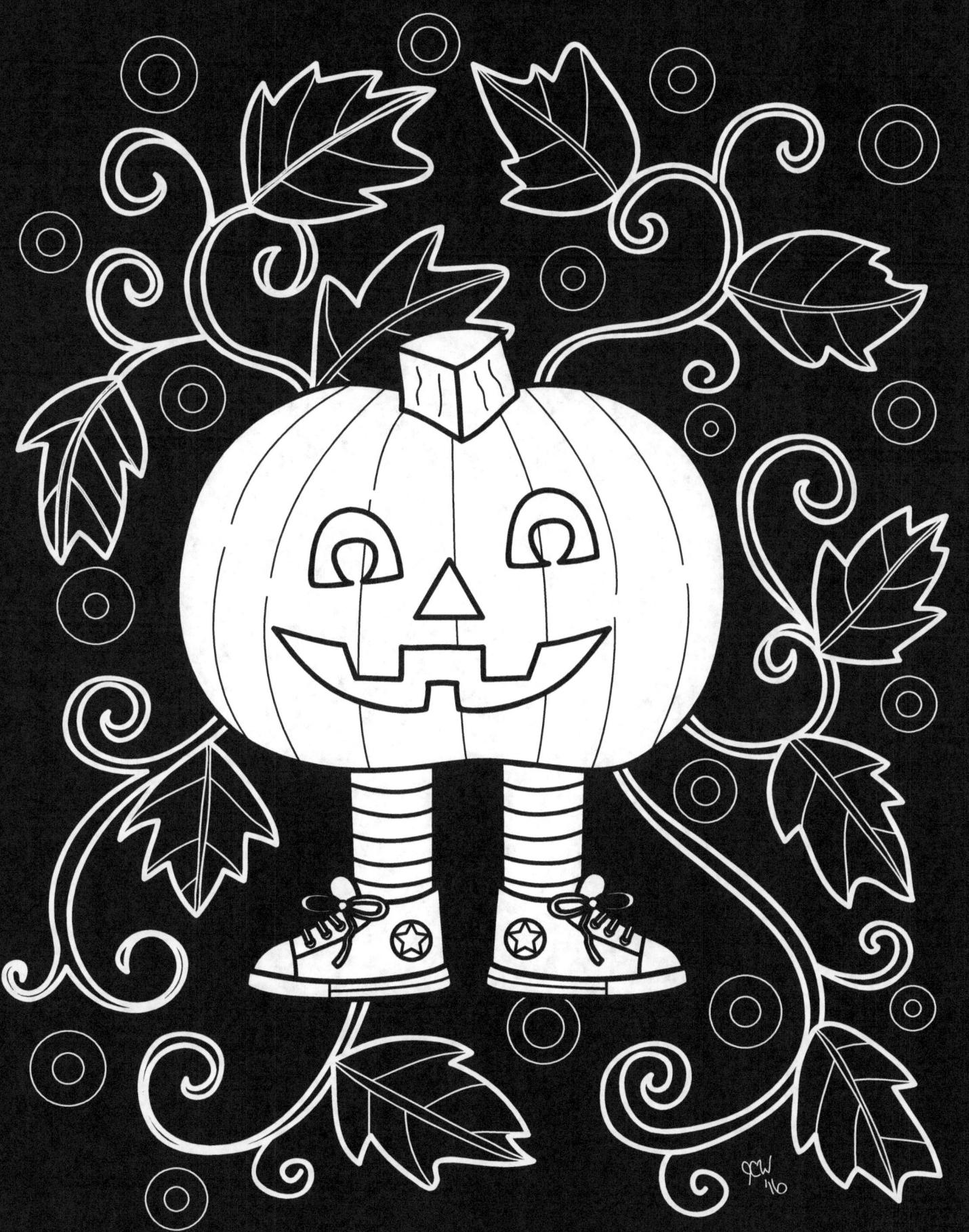

Want More?

Check out my other books and more on
Amazon and Etsy, and
www.TheRootsOfDesign.com

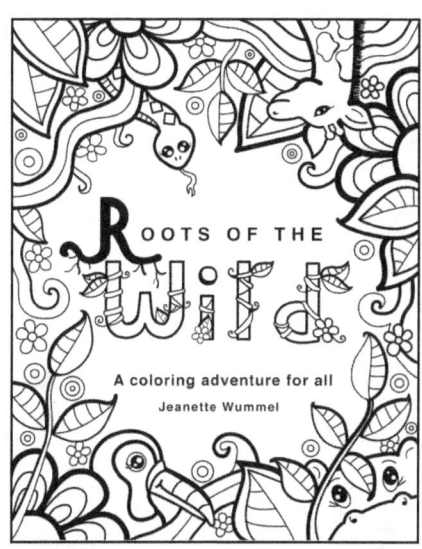

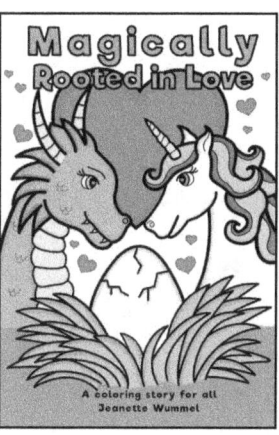

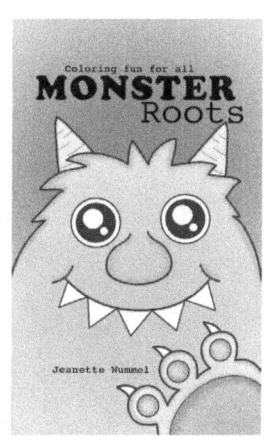

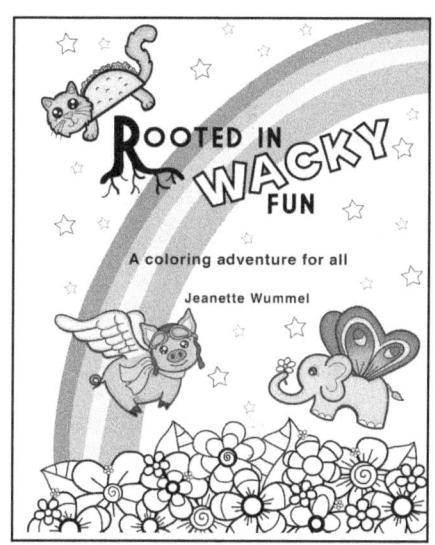

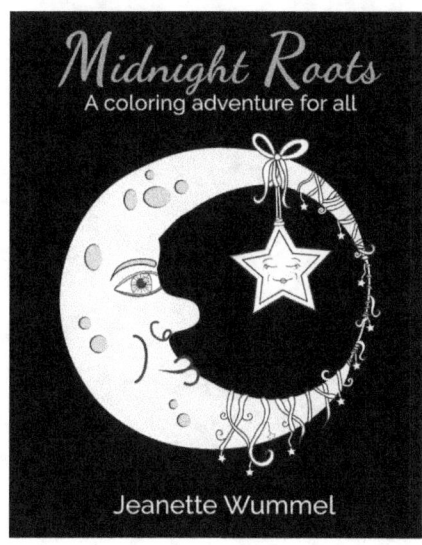

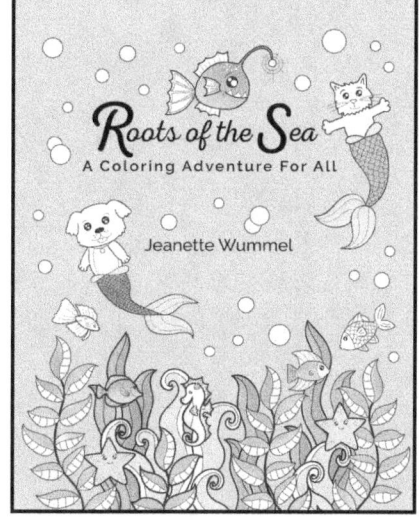

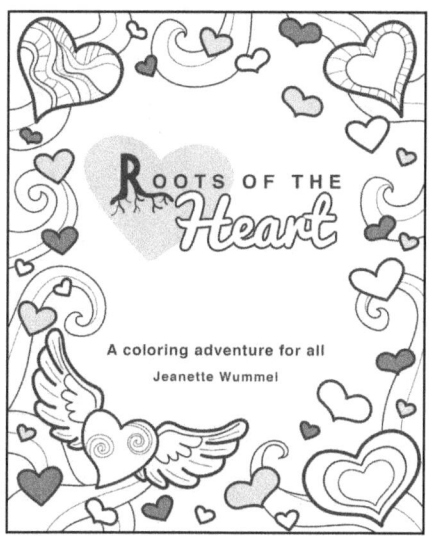

www.ingramcontent.com/pod-product-compliance
Lightning Source LLC
Chambersburg PA
CBHW080819170526
45158CB00009B/2468